A GUIDE FOR USE
IN PLANNING AND CONDUCTING
RESEARCH PROJECTS

A GUIDE FOR USE
IN PLANNING AND CONDUCTING
RESEARCH PROJECTS

By

PAUL WESTMEYER, Ed.D.

College of Multidisciplinary Studies
Division of Education
The University of Texas at San Antonio
San Antonio, Texas

CHARLES C THOMAS • PUBLISHER
Springfield • Illinois • U.S.A.

Published and Distributed Throughout the World by

CHARLES C THOMAS • PUBLISHER

Bannerstone House

301-327 East Lawrence Avenue, Springfield, Illinois, U.S.A.

©*1981, by* CHARLES C THOMAS • PUBLISHER

ISBN 0-398-04449-X

Library of Congress Catalog Card Number 80-27066

Library of Congress Cataloging in Publication Data

Westmeyer, Paul.
    A guide for use in planning and conducting research
projects.

    Includes index.
    1. Research--Methodology. I. Title.
Q180.55.M4W47   001.4'2   80-27066
ISBN 0-398-04449-X

Printed in the United States of America
AF-RX-1

HOW TO USE THIS GUIDE

This is a guide to planning and conducting research projects. As such, it will give you help in deciding upon a research problem, in stating hypotheses or questions to be answered, in planning for the collection of data, in actually writing a research proposal, in analyzing and interpreting data, and in writing the research report when the project is completed. It is not a book on research designs. (For these, if you want basic designs or elaborate ones, you should see a work such as that by Campbell and Stanley, which appeared as a chapter in the *Handbook of Research on Teaching*.)[1]

This is also not a book on statistical treatment of data. Many references are available for this purpose. What this guide does is suggest ways of organizing data for analysis and interpretation; for the specific statistical tests you will need to consult other references. Finally, this is not a book on "grantsmanship," although it does contain numerous hints on points that need to be considered when writing a proposal for the funding of research.

Here is how to use the guide:
• Read the Introduction. This tells you the definition of research that is used throughout the guide, and it gives you some "places to start" if you do not already have a research problem in mind.
• Once you have identified a problem area in which you would like to do research, examine the Contents page to see where you need to turn next for guidance.
• If you need help all the way through the project (if you are a novice at research — no offense intended), follow the guide right through chapter by chapter as you need each one.
• If you must prepare a proposal, whether it be for funding, for a thesis or dissertation, or for internal approval of faculty research, read Chapters 3 and 4 first. When you do this you may find that you need the guidance provided in Chapter 2 on planning your research, but first look at the guides to writing the proposal and find out what you need in addition to this.
• When you are ready to begin the literature search, whether this is for the proposal or for background required in the research project (getting started on the research project), you should read Chapter 1 because it provides some very specific guidelines that you might find useful in keeping your notes straight and in getting them interpreted into a chapter of the report later.
• In some cases your best beginning place might be Chapter 2 because what you really must think through first is the plan of action that you will follow in your research. This chapter provides that kind of guidance.
• Chapter 4 is a concise guide to writing a research proposal; it provides an

---

[1] N. L. *Gage, Handbook of Research on Teaching* (Chicago, Rand McNally and Company, 1963). Chapter Five of this work has been reprinted in Donald T. Campbell, Julian C. Stanley, *Experimental and Quasi-Experimental Designs for Research* (Chicago, Rand McNally and Company, 1966).

outline and a listing of the important things that need to be considered. If you already have your problem in mind and if you have basically decided on how you want to go about collecting data, you might want to read Chapter 4 right away and see where you need to go from there.

• Chapters 5 and 6 are the ones you need while you are doing the research. This means, of course, that you should read them through before beginning the actual collection of data and then follow their guidance as the project develops. If you are going to do historical or descriptive research, it may be particularly important to you to read these two chapters for the ideas they present on how to handle non-numerical data.

• Everyone, except experienced authors, can use guidance when it comes to writing a research report. If you have not written such a report before, you will find a lot of suggestions in the last chapter in this guide on how to prepare the manuscript so that it will be acceptable and useful. If you have written research reports before, you may still find some ideas for doing things differently that you may want to adapt from this chapter.

• Finally, why not mark up the book? Where a better idea occurs to you than what is suggested, why not write it in so that your next project can benefit from it? Write in the margins, insert pages, cut up the book, and make a loose-leaf package out of it so you can insert your own materials.

INTRODUCTION

An item appeared in newspapers in the fall of 1979 saying that a scientist had found out how robins locate earthworms.[1] What apparently had happened is that the scientist had observed that robins are seen pulling earthworms from the ground more frequently after a rain than they are at other times. He watered his lawn, got down on his hands and knees, and placed his chin on the ground (thus placing his eyes at about "robin's eye" level). Looking around, he saw earthworms; they were out in plain view to an eye low enough to observe them.

Was this research? Well, the man had a problem that he wanted to solve, which was, "How do robins locate earthworms?" He used the prior information that he had, the observation that earthworm-eating robins are more abundant after a rain than at other times. He arranged for the collection of additional data[2] by watering the lawn and looking for worms. He also solved the original problem to his satisfaction; he concluded that robins simply see the earthworms and that there is nothing mysterious about their location mechanism.

[1]*San Antonio Express* (San Antonio, Texas, Express-News Corporation, 10 Nov. 1979).
[2]Data is the plural of datum in Latin, but in English the word datum seems awkward and, in fact, is rarely used. Hence, data has come to be used in either the singular or the plural sense, depending on the context. As long ago as 1965, Gowers said in H.W. Fowler, *A Dictionary of Modern English Usage,* 2nd ed. Ed. by Ernest Gowers (New York and Oxford, Oxford University Press, 1965) that "data" was often treated as a singular word in America (though not in Britain). He also indicated that the correct pronunciation was data. In this guide "data" is usually treated as a singular word, but it may occasionally be considered plural if it seems to make more sense in context. Readers who are purists and want the word always to be singular or always to be plural are advised to mark up the guide accordingly.

Of course, in this research there was no sophisticated data analysis, no analysis of covariance, no regression calculations, not even a table of data, and it is unlikely that the scientist could get his results published in a scientific journal — at least not as a research article. But, he did get them published in a newspaper.

In another article, this one in a news publication for chemists,[3] a research plan was described in which some 2 million dollars would be spent and two years of time would be required just to construct the data-collecting apparatus. The problem was to determine whether or not protons decay into lighter particles, and the detector of such events would be a 10,000 ton body of water, 2000 feet underground, surrounded by some 2000 photomultiplier tubes. What would be observed with this device would not be protons disintegrating but rather some effect in the water ("tracks") that could only be explained by assuming that a proton had decayed.

The research would require sophisticated data analysis, it would include the collection of masses of information, and the results would almost certainly be published in respectable journals.

What do the two preceding research projects described briefly have in common?

1. A problem is stated for which there is not at present a solution.
2. Information already existing that is related to the problem is utilized in refining the problem and/or determining what type of additional data should be collected.
3. Procedures are designed, and the additional data needed is obtained.
4. The evidence collected is related to the original problem, and an answer is formulated as a solution for the problem.

The assumption in this book is that what constitutes research is carrying out the four steps listed here. This is not meant to rule out additional steps that might be required in some types of research or in some individual research projects; it is meant only to define research by describing the minimum requirements of a project, the minimum test to which the project is to be subjected, for determining whether it is research or not.

Why is the definition of research so carefully spelled out here? After all, the reader is convinced that what is to be done will be research, or this book would not be among the tools considered.

I'm going to start talking directly to you now; the language I have been using has been getting cumbersome, and I feel the need to change. I won't use "I" very often, and when I do I will put the material in this kind of type so that you will know that I am relating a personal experience or telling you a personal opinion that I feel might be of use. I will use "you" quite frequently, however, so that I can avoid talking about "the reader."

The reason that research is defined is that you will be reading a lot of published materials in the course of carrying out your research project, and it is vital for you to distinguish between published materials that report research findings and those which report the opinions of the author. If research has been properly conducted,

[3]*Chemical and Engineering News* (Washington, D.C., The American Chemical Society, 57:32, 15 Oct. 1979).

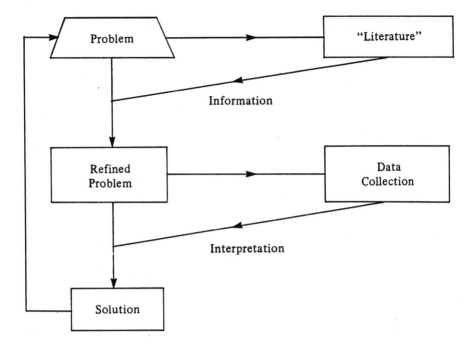

the findings cannot be ignored but must be taken into account if they have a bearing on your problem. On the other hand, opinions can be totally ignored with impunity; your opinion is as good as that of anyone else.

Well, the last statement isn't quite true. When the opinion in question is that of an expert in the field and you are not an equivalent expert, you would be unwise to ignore the opinion published. As a matter of fact, there will be cases in which you may have to use expert opinions as the data, or part of the data, to be used in solving your problem, but a research finding is a fact in the sense that it can be used as correct information in relation to another piece of research, while an opinion can never be reported as a fact, even though it might be used in carrying out a research project.

One of the most common problems that a researcher confronts is locating a problem to research. The graduate student faced with the necessity of producing a thesis or dissertation panics when he cannot think of a problem to research.[4] The young faculty member who realizes that he must do research (and publish) to be promoted and given tenure has a terrible time thinking of a problem to investigate. Locating a problem is not one of the major headings in this book. It is assumed either that you have a problem area already identified by the time you begin to use this book or that the following will provide enough guidance to let you get started. (Getting started is really all that is needed because selecting a problem is not what is important in research; what is important is defining a researchable problem and stating it in proper terms. So, you can see that all you need at first is a general area in

[4]In trying to keep things simple and not to clutter the text with avoidance of sexually biased statements or terms, the older form of terminology in which ''he'' refers to people in general has been used. The reader who is uncomfortable with this usage should mark up the book as with ''data'' so that he/she can read it in her/his own terms.

which you think you would like to do research. When you begin the literature search in this area, you will probably be able, rather quickly, to decide upon a specific question that you think needs to be answered. Then the refining begins.)

Where do you find a research area? If you are a graduate student, it may be as simple as having your professor assign you a problem area. Maybe you can talk to faculty members to find out what areas of research they are exploring. Then you can choose one of these areas that sounds interesting to you and interview the faculty member, asking for advice on needed research. Maybe you just need to think about your daily job for a while. Certainly there are aspects of the job in which there is a need for exploration. How could this be done better? Why is this procedure utilized; might there be a better one? How are decisions of this kind made? Where does the information come from? Is there a paradigm that describes the process of decision

making? What skills are needed by persons new to this field so that they can do the job required? On and on goes the analysis of a job; there are many research possibilities in any activity.

If you are a teacher, you have a triple opportunity for research. You can inquire into the subject matter you teach and perhaps conduct research that will add to the basic store of information. You can inquire into the teaching process. For example, if you did something differently, what would be the result? If the subject matter were presented in a different order, would learning be different? Can this be taught more efficiently by use of media than by lecture? Or, you can inquire into the nature of the learners and the interactions of learner and instructor. Is a given procedure more effective with slow learners than it is with fast learners? With students of a specific background, what is the most effective way to introduce this topic? What is the effect on students of teacher praise (or blame)? Do students with different cognitive styles react differently to teacher actions?

Practically every student who has written a thesis or dissertation has been advised that he must include in it, as the final section, suggestions for further research. Thus, a very good source of ideas for research would be just these sections of theses. Look in dissertation or thesis listings for titles that sound as though they are in an area of interest to you. Then borrow the bound paper from the library and read the ''suggestions'' section. You do not have to take a suggestion as it is given; all you are looking for at this stage is an idea of where to begin.

A fourth way to locate a research problem area is to get involved in a seminar or colloquium series. If you are a graduate student, one of the best sources of ideas for research is your fellow students; for faculty members, the same is true of fellow faculty. The saying might be, ''Research breeds more research.'' As soon as you get involved in research in any way, even if it is only listening to others describe what they are doing or even if it is only reading research reports, you will begin to get ideas for things you would like to try yourself.

I'll tell you where I got the idea for my first research project — my master's thesis. I was doing graduate work in science education and taking courses in both biology and chemistry. Both areas had lots of intriguing problems, but I had found none that I really wanted to tackle. As part of the degree program, I also was taking a course on how to do educational research. The course was taught by the man who was responsible for accepting theses at the university, and one day in class he was describing the areas of research that he considered acceptable and unacceptable. In trying to make a joke he said, "I don't want you just to go into a cornfield out in the state (with a partner) and tell me you have been doing research." It struck me all of a sudden that there were many, many cornfields in the state that had been abandoned — people just stopped farming them when they were no longer as productive as they had been. One of the biology courses that I had really enjoyed was ecology, and one of the major themes in ecology is plant succession, the sequence of dominant plants or plant communities that develops on soil which is not disturbed. So, I said to myself, "What I want to do is to determine the plant succession on these abandoned farmlands." I'll probably tell you more of this project as you read through this book, but for now, I'm just interested in telling you how I got the idea for it.

So, it is assumed that you have a problem area in which you plan to do research. You do not need to have the problem itself already defined and stated in good research terms; this book will help you do that, as well as help you plan and conduct the rest of the project.

ACKNOWLEDGMENTS

Since I teach research methods, I am indebted to all of the students who have participated in my classes for their contributions to my own thinking about research. Ideas do become much clearer when you try to communicate them to others. The fabulous artist who drew the cartoons used in this book is the mother of one of these students. The artist is Algire Leister. She has both a B.F.A. and an M.F.A. in the teaching of art from Maryland Institute; she lives in Annapolis, Maryland. The idea for the very last cartoon in the book was suggested by another student of mine, Chuck Janzow.

Finally, as for all authors (or at least most of us), I am indebted to my wife and family for the time they allowed me to spend away from home working on this manuscript.

To all of the above my thanks.

CONTENTS

A GUIDE FOR USE
IN PLANNING AND CONDUCTING
RESEARCH PROJECTS

Chapter 1

THE LITERATURE SEARCH

Before any experimentation is begun, the researcher must do a litera-ture search. This is true in any field of study, and it is true regardless of how convinced you are in your own mind that your problem is unique and uninves-tigated. You see, the literature search has many purposes, among them (but only one among many) making sure that the problem that you want to investi-gate has not already been solved. Furthermore, you need to do the literature search before you submit your proposal for research to whoever has to ap-prove it. Once you have chosen the problem area, the next thing you need to do is to search the literature for related information. As you do this you are looking for the following:

1. Material that suggests that the problem has already been solved
2. Evidence that may suggest that some aspects of the problem or of re-lated problems have been solved
3. Suggestions that within the problem area you have chosen there are indeed questions which other people have said need to be answered
4. Hints that there might be some relatively specific questions which are more important than others, perhaps questions whose answers would suggest answers to still other questions
5. Ideas on how to go about conducting research on the question you have in mind, research designs
6. Instruments that might be useful in data collection, or observation techniques that you might be able to adapt
7. Statistical or analytical tools that you might be able to use or adapt
8. Specific information (that is, data) that bears on the problem you want to investigate
9. Names of other researchers who are working in the same or related areas (in case you need to contact someone for help)
10. Sources of additional information (primarily gleaned from the bib-liographies of the research articles you read)

Of course, you will take notes as you read articles and books on your prob-lem. You probably ought to devise for yourself some sort of coding system for your notes so that you can quickly identify later, when you have read so many materials that they all run together in your mind, those which are relevant to each of the items listed previously. You could just use the numbers in the lower left corner of each note card, or you could devise a more elaborate system.

LOCATING THE LITERATURE SOURCES

To begin your literature search, you first need a list of descriptors, key words or terms that you will look for in card catalogs (to locate books), in indexes (to locate chapters or sections within books), in guides to journal publications (to locate articles), and in asking your librarian for help. Depending on what the field of your research is, you might be able to find a thesaurus that lists commonly used descriptors; ask your librarian. The Educational Resources Information Center (ERIC), which collects research information in a variety of fields of education and stores the articles in central locations, publishes such a thesaurus listing the descriptors used in ERIC records.[1]

Make a list of descriptors that you think will help you locate material related to your problem area. As you use the list, you will find other descriptors that you had not thought of, and you will find that some on your list are not used in the literature; modify the list as you go along, and keep it with you whenever you go to the library.

When I was doing the literature search for my thesis research problem, which was, "What is the succession of plants on abandoned farmlands in southeastern Indiana?", I had a list of descriptors that included succession, plant succession, fields, abandoned fields, cultivation, dominant, climax, ecology, and others. Notice that some descriptors should be quite specific to the problem at hand, and others should be very general so that you can get a broad view of what has been written on the topic.

Card Catalog

You should start with the card catalog (often nowadays a filmed catalog rather than actual cards), which lists books by author, title, and subject. You may not want to read the books you find first in your literature search, but you should identify them, locate them, and at least skim through them to see what kind of information you will find there. You may find one or more summaries of research in this process, and these may at least lead you to original sources if you do not feel that you can trust the summarizers for the information provided.[2]

---

[1]*Thesaurus of ERIC Descriptors* (New York; CCM Information Corporation, 1970).
[2]*The American Educational Research Association* has published such summaries since 1931, called *Review of Educational Research* for a given year.

Now, don't go very far into the process of locating references and reading them before you read a later section in this book on abstracting or taking notes; I have some very specific suggestions for you on how to keep a record of your readings so that you will be able to put together the literature search section of your proposal and/or research report with relative ease.

Periodical Indexes

The second general listing you will want to look at is whatever periodical indexes apply to your topic. The most general (and oldest) index is the *Readers' Guide to Periodical Literature* (New York, H. W. Wilson Co., 950 University Avenue, The Bronx). This guide provides an index to articles in over 100 magazines, not research journals, and so may not be a very good source of information for your project. It is worth looking at, however, in the early stages of your work.

Some indexes published for specific areas are the following:

Art Index (New York, H. W. Wilson Co., 950 University Avenue, The Bronx).

Bioresearch Index (Philadelphia, BioSciences Information Service, 2100 Arch Avenue).

Education Index (New York, H. W. Wilson Co., 950 University Avenue, The Bronx).

Social Science Citation Index (Philadelphia, Institute for Scientific Information, 325 Chestnut Street).

This is not a complete listing by any means; check your library for the indexes available there, and ask the reference librarian for help if you need it.

Published Abstracts

The sources suggested so far lead you to original information, that is, information provided directly to you from the person who first learned it. As much as possible, you should use this firsthand information in your literature search. However, there is another way to get to such original sources, and that is to go through published abstracts. The abstract publication that is perhaps most closely tied to the original sources is *Dissertation Abstracts International*.[3] The abstracts in this publication are written by the dissertation authors themselves rather than by a second party. You can, of course, read the abstracts of dissertations that sound as if they might be related to your problem. Then, if you find some that you really want to use, you can obtain microfilm or printed copies of the original through your librarian.

In many subject areas there are abstracting services that summarize research which has been reported. Usually this service has been set up because the research in the area is so abundant that an individual would find it impossible to keep up with it if there were not abstracts, instead of whole articles, available to him. Some (but by no means all) of these abstract services are the following:

[3]*Dissertation Abstracts International* (Ann Arbor, Mich., University Microfilms).

Abstracts in Anthropology (Farmingdale, N.Y., Baywood Publishing Co., Inc., 120 Marine Street).

Biological Abstracts (Philadelphia, BioSciences Information Service, 2100 Arch Street).

Chemical Abstracts (Columbus, Ohio, Chemical Abstracts Service, American Chemical Society, 2540 Olentangy River Road).

Physics Abstracts (Surrey, England, Institution of Electrical Engineers, Unwin Brothers, Ltd. Old Woking).

Psychological Abstracts (Washington, American Psychological Association, Inc., 1200 Seventeenth Street, N.W.).

Sociological Abstracts (San Diego, Sociological Abstracts, Inc., P.O. Box 22206).

One that is a little different in format in that it combines indexing and abstracting in one publication is *Current Index to Journals in Education* (New York, CCM Information Corporation). Please read also the section in this chapter on ERIC.

Research In Progress

Often you may want to find out if someone might be currently working on a research problem similar to yours; the research will not have been published yet, of course, so you cannot locate it in any of the sources listed previously. Many professional societies provide, as a service to their members, lists of research projects in progress. Check with experts in your field to find out if there is such a list available.

Much research is funded by the federal government, and information on such research underway is available through the *Smithsonian Science Information Exchange*.[4] This is a kind of index that lists research projects by subject, location, and name of the researcher. It also provides a brief description of the problem and procedures and indicates the current status, e.g. just begun, second year, etc.

Another publication similar to the preceding one, but limited to the field of education, is called *Research in Education*.[5] This is a monthly publication, which lists and describes (i.e. abstracts) research in progress and/or completed that has been funded by the United States Office of Education. This is a part of the ERIC service; see the following section for a description of ERIC.

Educational Resources Information Center (ERIC)

For researchers in education, the United States Office of Education has established what is perhaps the single most useful tool one could imagine. The Educational Resources Information Center has been set up with a central of-

[4]Smithsonian Science Information Exchange, Inc., Room 300, 1830 M Street, N. W., Washington, D.C. 20036.

[5]Research in Education (Washington, D.C., United States Office of Education).

fice and a number of separate clearinghouses, each representing a different segment of the large field of education. (For example, there are clearinghouses for science education, vocational and technical education, teacher education, and many others.) In these clearinghouses, ERIC collects research reports from whatever source they are available, not only articles but also papers presented at professional meetings, for example, project reports and whatever reports authors send in. The success of an ERIC depends largely upon authors of research reports getting them to the clearinghouse. At the clearinghouse each report is abstracted, indexed, identified with an accession number, and microfilmed. From this film record, then, you can obtain either a microfiche copy of the original document or a printed copy if you prefer. Indeed, your library may have the microfiche ERIC materials on file.

The ERIC clearinghouses publish annotated bibliographies, and one of these might help solve your problem of locating recent research in areas related to your study. If not, you may want to use the ERIC computer search (see the next section in this chapter).

By the way, if your research is related to education, do send a copy of the report to the appropriate ERIC clearinghouse after the project is finished. Also, ask your librarian for a copy of *How to Use ERIC*.

Computer Search Services

It really is very time-consuming to conduct a personal search of the literature as described so far in this chapter. Nevertheless, if you have a problem area that is relatively easy to define, and if it is rather limited in scope, you may want to conduct the search yourself. If the problem area is "loose" and broad, however, you may want to use a computer service to help you locate likely literature sources. (This will be more expensive, of course, but it usually is not unreasonable.) No doubt you will need the help of your reference librarian, so do not hestitate to ask, early in the course of your project, what computer search service might be available and how much it would cost.

All the ERIC materials are accessible through the DIALOG® computer system (Lockheed) and the SDC/ORBIT® system. In addition, *Psychological Abstracts* materials, *Dissertation Abstracts,* and *Smithsonian Science Information Exchange* materials, among those that have been mentioned in this chapter, are available to computer search mechanisms. No doubt many of the other sources also are available to such computer search systems or will have become available to them by the time you are reading this manual. Essentially, what you need to do in order to use a computer search is the following.

First, you need to have the problem rather well defined. This means that you need to do a preliminary search of the literature on your own, going at least as far as is necessary to define an actual problem (as opposed to a problem area, which is what this chapter has dealt with so far).

Second, you need to establish a list of descriptors to be used in the search. These are what the computer will search for in its indices, and what you will get from the computer is a list of all articles for which the descriptors chosen were used when they were indexed. Think over very carefully what terms will describe the kind of research information you are looking for, then ask your librarian to help suggest the proper way of stating each term for a computer search. In the actual search you can, of course, combine descriptors so that articles that have been indexed under the combination are the only ones that will be listed for you. Suppose, for example, that you are interested in studying the possible effects of level of reading comprehension in science on actual science achievement in seventh grade students. You will not need to have a list of all articles that have been published on reading comprehension, nor will you need all articles related to achievement in science. What you want is the combination of reading comprehension and science achievement, so you can combine the two descriptors (with ''and'') for your literature search. Should you also combine a third descriptor, the grade level or perhaps the general grade level (middle school)? Probably you should not do so because it is quite likely that research that has examined the possible relationship of reading comprehension and science achievement at any level will have some bearing on your problem in this case. Besides, if you specify three or more descriptors to be met simultaneously you are very severely limiting the number of sources that will be listed.

Third, you need to tell the computer what sources of information to search (ERIC, *Psychological Abstracts, Chemical Abstracts,* or whatever).

Fourth, you can limit the search to either a specific set of years, e.g. from 1965 to present, or a specific number of listings, e.g. the 30 most recent articles. Of course, you can allow the search to cover all the recorded information.

From here it is up to you if you are going to use a computer search for help in locating appropriate research reports from the literature. I cannot guide you in doing the search because procedures depend upon what is available to you in your library. You can get a search done by mail, at least in selected areas.[6] Should you desire to use the computer in doing your first search, before the problem is defined, this is all right too. You will use broader descriptors and, no doubt, get longer lists of articles from which you will try to choose those which fit what you require. I recommend heavy dependence on your reference librarian at this point.

ABSTRACTING OR TAKING NOTES

Most researchers use cards to take notes as they read materials to which they will refer in their studies. There is nothing magic about notes on cards, however. All you need is to have your notes for each research report on a

[6]Contact University Microfilms, 300 North Zeeb Road, Ann Arbor, Michigan 48106.

separate piece of paper from the notes for other reports so that you can shuffle the notes when you are ready to write the literature search section of your own report or proposal. One of the handiest ways to carry note materials is the bound card "books" (loose-leaf binding) now commonly available. Using one of these, you have the flexibility of having individual cards and also the security of having all the materials bound together.

With the availability of copying machines, many researchers also prefer to make copies of the material that they want from articles and books and to work directly from these copies later. This is fine too, but eventually you will need to condense and/or paraphrase contents from your notes or copied materials, so the following sections provide guidance on how to do this.

Personally, I recommend that you use copy machines to duplicate pages from books, tables of data, complicated formulas, and the like that you might want for later use. But, I don't recommend copying research reports or articles. What I think you should do in this case is to abstract the material directly on your note cards; in other words, take notes in the form of abstracts rather than in the loose narrative or semiquoted form commonly utilized.

Noting Bibliographic Information

Never take notes of any kind or copy materials without at the same time making note of the complete bibliographic information that describes the source. The format, of course, may vary, depending on the requirements of your "publisher." (If you are writing a thesis or dissertation, the university probably has a style manual that will specify bibliography format; if you are writing for a journal, there is also available a style guide in most instances.) But, in any event you need the following: (1) the author, (2) the title of the book, article, or report, (3) the name of the journal if it is an article that you are abstracting, (4) the publisher and place of publication, (5) the identifying reference for the specific source you are using — the edition for a book, the volume number for a journal, the report number for a research report, the project number for a project report, etc., (6) the year in which the material was copyrighted, and (7) the page on which you found the reference you are paraphrasing or quoting.

Some examples follow (remember that you may be required to use a format other than the one shown here).

A Book

Westmeyer, Paul. *Successful Devices in Teaching Chemistry.* J. Weston Walch, Publisher, Portland, Maine. *Revised Edition,* 1975. p. 47.

A Curriculum Guide

Westmeyer, Paul (supervisor, with contributors). *Elementary Science Curriculum Guide, Grades K–5.* San Antonio Independent School District, San Antonio, Texas. 1979. pp. 17 – 23.

A Research Report

Westmeyer, Paul, E. Brakken, and P. Fordyce. *A Comparison of Various Techniques for the Dissemination of a New Science Curriculum in Florida*. U.S. Department of Health, Education, and Welfare; Office of Education; Bureau of Research. March 1967. p. 31. (Note that this example report does not have an identifying number; most do, particularly if they were produced by a university or by an industry.)

A Thesis

Westmeyer, Paul. "Some Aspects of Plant Succession on Abandoned Farm Lands of Southeastern Indiana." Unpublished master's thesis. Ball State University, Muncie, Indiana. August 1952. p. 14.

A Journal Article

Espejo, Mila, P. Westmeyer, and R. Good. "Evaluation of a Child-Structured Science Curriculum Using the Intellectual Models of Piaget and Guilford." *Journal of Research in Science Teaching*. Vol. 12, No. 2, April 1975. pp. 147 – 155.

A Speech

Westmeyer, Paul. "The Flight from Science." Presidential address for AETS, given at New York City convention. April 1972. Published in *Convention Addresses*, NSTA, 1201 16th Street, N.W. Washington, D.C.

An Experiment Published in a Collection

Westmeyer, Paul. "Finding Molecular Weights." Published in *Scientific Experiments in Chemistry, Student Guide*. Manufacturing Chemists Association, Inc., 1625 Eye Avenue, N. W., Washington, D.C. 1958, pp. 47 and 48.

Author
Title of book, article or report
     Journal (for articles)
Publisher and location
Identifying Reference
     (book edition, journal volume and number, report number, project number, etc.)
Copyright date
Page(s) on which abstracted information was found

Abstracting

Remember that you will be abstracting research reports or research articles primarily. (If you are doing a historical study and using literature as the source of data, you may be going far beyond this, but for the present, think in terms of making a record of the information you want to use from research articles.) The pertinent parts of the report that you need to locate and describe in your own terms are as follows.

1. The Problem

State the problem, as a question or as an hypothesis. Describe any context or setting that makes the problem unique, if there is any.

2. The Design

Describe the design in standard terms, e.g. a factorial study with two conditions for variable A and three for variable B, and add any description that sets this design apart from the standard. Record the method of sampling and the size of the sample. Identify the population or reference to which findings will be generalized. Describe controls.

3. Information Regarding Data Collection

What was the nature of the data? What instruments or devices were used? Describe validity and reliability. What process was followed, e.g. if observers were used, was interobserver reliability established? How? When and where were the data collected?

4. Data Analysis

Describe the organization of data and any statistical techniques that were used. What level of significance was set?

5. Findings and/or Conclusions

Record the results of the study, the relationship between the original problem and the findings, conclusions drawn by the author, etc.

A sample abstract of an imaginary study (but based on some real information) follows.

> Smith, Buford J. and Samuel Donegan. "Analysis of the school performance of children weighing less than five pounds at birth compared with that of children weighing five pounds or greater at birth." *Journal of Applied Medical Research.* Vol. 22, No. 1, January 1975. pp. 17 – 23.
>
> As part of a larger question regarding the effects of prenatal nutrition on the intellectual development of children, an answer was sought to the question, Are premature babies handicapped in their eventual school performance? Birth records at the University of Minnesota Research Hospital were examined in order to identify some 1000 children born between 1960 and 1973 who could be traced and for whom school records could be obtained. Point biserial correlation coefficients were calculated between birth weight (i.e. premature versus nonpremature babies) and each of IQ at age five, IQ at age seven, achievement at age seven in language, reading, spelling, and arithmetic, in this ex post facto, correlational study. Chi square analysis was also used to determine whether or not there were any differences between the two groups with regard to retention in grade in school. All analyses showed the low birth weight children to be inferior to their heavier peers at the .05 level of significance. A follow-up study was made to determine whether the decisive factor was length of term of gestation or birth weight per se, with the finding in favor of the latter, again at the .05 level of significance. Fitting these findings into the larger picture suggests that prenatal nutrition may indeed be a significant factor in the school success of children.

This kind of abstract will provide what is needed for most of the articles to be used later in reporting the literature search, but it does not include specific information that you might want for other purposes in your study. Therefore, you might want to include the following additional categories of content for selected abstracts.

6. Justification or Clarification

Record any parts of the article or report that contribute to a clarification of your research area, that indicate that the research you want to do is important and needed, or that suggest ways in which your research problem might be refined or limited.

7. Unique Design Ideas

If you locate a study in which some procedure or element of design was altered from the standard in ways that you might want to use yourself, record that fact so that you can eventually give proper credit to the originator.

8. Data Handling

As in the preceding item, you may find unique ways of locating, collecting, analyzing, or interpreting data. If these represent something that you think you might be able to use, record them with the abstract.

9. Specific Information

Certainly if you are doing historical research, you will record specific information from the literature read, but this might also be true in other types of research. You may find an item of data that has a direct bearing on the problem you are trying to solve or a fact that you may need to have later. By all means record these with the abstract.

10. Anything Else That Might Be of Use

Record names and addresses of other researchers with whom you might want to correspond, bibliographic references cited in articles that sound as if they might be useful to you, names and sources of tests or measuring instruments used, and whatever else appears as though it might be useful in your study.

When I began the research for my doctoral dissertation, in conducting the literature search, I ran across a reference to a test called "The Whole Truth and Nothing But the Truth Test in Chemistry." I recorded the reference, looked it up later, and identified the author of the test. I wrote to the author and asked about the test. He told me that the test was about to be published but that if I wanted he would send me a copy in advance. When I got the test, it looked so intriguing and fit what I was trying to measure so well that I asked permission to reproduce it (since it was not in print yet) and used it as one of the measures in my own research.

A Word About Copying Copyrighted Materials

If in the course of your taking notes you decide to shorten some of the library time by making machine copies of materials you want to use, be aware of the possible infringement of copyright in doing so. In general, it is proper and legal to make copies of material for use in research if, by doing so, you are not avoiding the purchase of such materials with benefit to the publisher. For example, you could make a machine copy of a test in order to quote from it or use parts of it as examples in a dissertation, but if you made multiple copies of it and used it as one of the measuring instruments in your study, you would be violating the copyright. In the latter case you should purchase the copies needed from the publisher, and making your own machine copies would deny the publisher a certain amount of income to which he is entitled.

You could also be violating copyright if you copied too much of a book or journal. The general rule is that you may copy (for use in research but not for commercial use) a chapter from a book (notice the limit); an article from a periodical (but if you copy a second article, you really ought to purchase the periodical instead); a short story, essay, or poem; a chart, diagram, drawing, cartoon, or picture (but, again, if you copy more than one you really ought to purchase a copy of the book or periodical instead of making the copy).

If in doubt, do not make the copy; buy the journal.

As a matter of fact, even my previous suggestion that you might legitimately copy a test for the purposes described is borderline. It may be that you should purchase the single copy of the test required instead of copying it. I guess what I really had in mind was copying a test that is published in the context of an article or book, in which case the rule above would let you make the single copy.

INTERPRETING AND ORGANIZING YOUR NOTES

If you made coded notations on your note cards, as suggested earlier, organizing the notes will now be fairly easy. You may want to go to the trouble of duplicating those note cards on which you had made two or more code marks so that you can place a set of notes into each category; it will simplify the writing of the literature search. At any rate, what you need to do first is to categorize the notes into the ten kinds of materials identified at the very beginning of this chapter.

Next, take a look at categories nine and ten and decide whether you need to follow up on anything in your notes there before going ahead with the interpretation of your literature notes.

Lay aside your notes in categories five, six, and seven; you will not need these until later.

Examine what you have written in category eight. Some material here might be useful later; this can be laid aside for now. Other material in category eight may be needed now. Keep this set in mind as you do the following.

Consider categories one, two, three, and four with the purpose of deciding exactly what the problem in your research project will be. If what you originally had in mind has already been solved (category one notes) you need to look at the possibility of working on a related problem (category two) or choosing a limited aspect of the original problem (category two and category three considered together). Adding your notes from category four to what you have already considered should let you narrow the research to a single question that still (after reviewing all of the literature) appears to you to be (1) important, (2) unsolved, (3) of interest to you, and (4) solvable within the limits of your capabilities and resources.

Those are the criteria for a good research problem. Notice that the first two are related to what you found in the literature, while the last two depend on your personal judgment.

I have to add a couple of other criteria that you really need to consider in addition to the ideal ones listed. If you are a student, you will have to convince your major professor, and possibly a committee, that the problem you want to work on is a good one. Presumably, you had this in mind when you started the literature search and were examining an *area* in which you knew your professor would be interested. If you want to publish the results of your research, you certainly cannot ignore the fact that certain kinds of studies in your field are "popular," while others are not. If you are considering obtaining a grant to support your research, again, you cannot ignore the fact that certain areas have more funds available to them than do others. When I was considering the problem of my own dissertation, what I really wanted to do was to develop and validate some curriculum materials for use in high school chemistry and a unique procedure for using them. What I found available was funds to support research related to the better utilization of teacher time in the classroom. So, I cast the problem in terms of better use through the method and materials I planned to develop — and received the needed funding. Do not compromise your ethics, but do be reasonable in considering possible changes in your basic ideas.

So, hopefully your literature search has led you to a single question that you can now investigate. If it has not and you have two or three questions, *avoid at all costs* putting all of them into your problem description. You *must* choose among them so that you end up with a single question to be examined. It is all right to have a problem with subproblem areas if you are very sure that they are subproblems to the major one and not just related questions that you want to examine. *When* you have narrowed your questions to one, proceed to the chapter on planning your research and to the section on stating the problem if you need help in doing this.

CHAPTER 2

PLANNING YOUR RESEARCH

$\mathbf{I}$n a (paraphrased) item in the *Chemical and Engineering News,*[1] it was reported that the absorption of zinc by the intestines is affected by the amount of pyridoxine (vitamin B^6) present. Specifically, the report said that when rats were given large doses of B^6 along with normal diet levels of zinc, they absorbed 71 percent of the zinc, whereas when rats were given small doses of B^6 along with the normal amount of zinc, they absorbed only 46 percent of the zinc. It was also reported that "large doses" meant 40 mg per kg of body weight and "small doses" meant 2 mg per kg of body weight. It is not important why anyone wanted to know this; the important question is, How was the research that led to this conclusion carried out? More to the point, How was this research designed or planned?

First, there was one or more literature searches involved so that before the research was planned the researcher knew that the question had not already been answered. But, there is another important point, that is, Why would anyone associate pyridoxine with zinc? (You might also wonder whether the findings, which are true for rats, can be extended to include humans. This question will be answered later.)

If you were to guess, and that is all that can be done at this point, you might assume that all the vitamins were considered potential correlates with the absorption of zinc and that, when a research study was carried out, B^6 emerged as *the* one. Suppose the researcher had started out with the question, How is zinc absorbed into the body? This might have led to the speculation that, as with most food absorption, certain chemicals would be found which direct the absorption in some way. If anything in the literature pointed toward vitamins as possibilities for such chemicals, a reasonable procedure would be to design an experiment to test this idea, with zinc as the material absorbed and each of the vitamins as cofactors to be examined. The experiment would probably be designed with a standard, and probably large, dose of each vitamin to accompany a standard dose of zinc in a sample of organisms. The researcher then would decide what organisms to use, what a standard dose means for each chemical , how the doses should be administered, etc. He would also have to

[1] "Zinc Uptake Increased by Vitamin B⁶," *Chemical and Engineering News, 57:* 24, 10 Dec. 1979.

determine how to measure the amount of zinc absorbed, and he would have to ask himself many other questions and get their answers before he could conduct the experiment that eventually would lead to the finding stated earlier.

The rest of this chapter deals with the usual sequence of events that you will have to go through in planning your research. You may not have to use all of them.

STATING THE PROBLEM

The last chapter made the point that you should begin with a single question as the problem of your research. This problem, at the beginning, should be in the form, "I wonder what would happen if . . ." Such a problem statement in connection with the vitamin research discussed previously might have been, "I wonder whether any of the vitamins has an effect on the absorption of zinc." However, a statement in this form is essentially unresearchable. What you need to do is to cast the problem into a form such that —

1. a relationship between two variables, or possibly among several variables, is questioned
2. each variable is operationally defined, either within the problem statement or in supplementary statements to it
3. a population, or in some cases the conditions, for the experiment is identified
4. the question is not trivial but will have some importance when answered
5. the action suggested by the problem statement is possible

Stating a Relationship

Suppose that the basic question a researcher has is, "If I allow children to watch all the violent shows on television that they would like to watch, will they become more violent themselves?" In a way, he has already expressed a relationship between two variables, violence on television and violence in children. However, what is meant by "violence" in each case has not been defined.

Research has been done on the effects of tea with lemon juice on polystyrene cups.[2] Someone noticed that when tea with lemon was placed in a polystyrene cup the cup leaked and he wondered what the effect of the tea with lemon was on the material of the cup. You could state the initial question in this case the following way: "I wonder what effect tea with lemon has on a polystyrene cup." In this question you have only vaguely implied a relationship between two variables, but if you stated your second level question as follows:

[2]K.M. Reese, "Lemon Tea in Polystyrene Cups Creates No Hazard," (Newscripts column) *Chemical and Engineering News, 57:*66, 24 Dec. 1979.

Does tea with lemon dissolve polystyrene?'' you have specified a relationship (dissolving) between two potential variables, tea with lemon as the supposed solvent and polystyrene as the supposed solute. If this last point confuses you, think of it this way: Does adding lemon to tea in a polystyrene cup affect the nature of the polystyrene by causing it to dissolve? It is clearer in this question that the manipulated variable is the nature of the liquid in the cup and the dependent variable is the nature of the polystyrene cup. The questioned *relationship* is whether or not the liquid dissolves the cup under specified conditions.

VARIABLES

In the preceding section variables were discussed without having been defined. A variable is anything or any condition that can exist in one form or state at a given time and in a different form or state at another time. It might also be thought of (in the case of people) as a characteristic that is different in one person than it is in another. Thus, height is a variable and so are age, hair color, eye color, intelligence, hand preference, and many other characteristics. Time is a variable; it can be long or short. Chemical state is a variable; substances are crystalline, dissolved, amorphous, etc. If you think of an experiment in which you teach a given set of materials by a specified process and then teach them to a different group by a process different from the first, the variable involved is *teaching process;* it is different from one time to another. What is the second variable in this case? This depends on what you specify in your problem statement, but it would probably be student achievement. What you would probably be interested in would be, ''Does the first or the second method produce better results in terms of student learning (achievement)?''

Variables are of several different kinds. A variable that you manipulate, that you change deliberately from one setting to another, is called a *manipulated variable* or, commonly, an *independent variable*. A variable that changes as a result of your manipulating the first variable is called a *dependent variable* (because its changes depend on changes in the first variable). When two variables change simultaneously but it is not possible to say that changes in one cause changes in the other, they can be called *co-variables*.

In some studies there may be two or more variables that have an effect on still another variable. Ordinarily only one of these is actually manipulated while the other(s) varies because of the nature of subjects. For example, in the teaching experiment just mentioned, where the procedures were varied, the ages of learners might also be different (say that you taught some sixth graders and some seventh graders the same materials by the same two processes). You cannot manipulate the age variable in this case — it varies because of the nature of the subjects. Such variables are called *assigned variables* if they are recognized as having some importance in a given experiment. Sometimes these variables are called ''organismic'' because they have to do with the existing nature of a subject, and sometimes they are called *moderator variables* because their action is to moderate the effect of the manipulated variable on the dependent variable. (In the example, the teaching process used first may be the better one for seventh graders, but the second process might be the better one for sixth graders. Age, then, would have been a moderator variable.)

There are also *control* (or controlled) *variables* and *innocuous variables*. The gas laws in chemistry illustrate controlled variables. At constant temperature, the volume of a confined gas varies inversely with the pressure in the container. At constant pressure, the volume of a confined gas varies directly with the temperature of the gas. In the first case, temperature is a controlled variable, and in the second, pressure is the controlled variable. Each is held constant so that it can have no effect on volume while the effect of the other (manipulated) variable is measured. An innocuous variable is what the term implies — one that is identifiable but has no effect. For example, hair color probably has no effect on reading ability.

RELATIONSHIPS BETWEEN VARIABLES

Variables can be related in the following ways:
1. cause and effect. Changing one variable (the independent or manipulated variable) causes a second one to change (the dependent variable).
2. predictor and predicted. Observing changes in one variable may enable you to predict what will eventually happen to the second, even though the changes in the first variable may not *cause* the changes in the second.
3. correlation. Two variables change concurrently, but neither can be said to cause changes in the other. It is obvious that there is overlapping among these conditions. Certainly if a given variable is a cause, it can then be used to predict changes in its dependent variable. Simultaneously, the two will be found to be correlated. Also, predictor and predicted variables must be correlated. The third category is used to cover precisely those cases in which neither of the other two exists; a good example of this is height and foot size in people. Certainly neither causes the other to vary. Also, you might be able to predict height if you knew foot size for an unseen individual, but you could also predict foot size if you knew height. See diagram on page 17.

What you need to do in stating your research problem is to describe one of the three relationships between the two variables you have identified. Sometimes this is straightforward: Will adding lemon to tea in a polystyrene cup *cause* changes in the nature of the cup? Specifically, will the polystyrene dissolve? Sometimes it is not nearly as clear. Try stating the relationship between variables in the earthworm and robin research mentioned in the Introduction.[3]

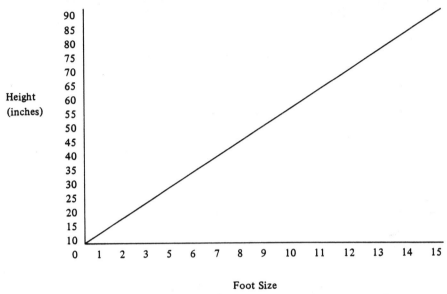

Foot Size

Defining Variables Operationally

You often hear that it is impossible to define love, ambition, taste, sensitivity, or other abstract ideas. However, you can define *anything* if you will specify how it will be measured. You could define love by saying that it is "measured by the number of times in a fifteen minute period the individual being observed uses a positive adjective to describe in any way the other person." You could define taste by measuring it "as the number of items found in this person's study that are identified by a panel of experts as being tasteful." Not everyone will agree with your definition; you have, nevertheless, defined the term.

Dissolving is a measurable process, so stating the problem in the tea with lemon study in terms of dissolving has specified an operation that is to be used in the study. It does not say how dissolving is to be measured, but there are standard processes for doing this.

To return to the violence on television problem, you could define television violence by identifying a specific set of TV movie scenes. Then the *measure*

[3]What you would *say* is, "Do robins locate earthworms by sight or by some other sense or process?" When you think in tems of variables, however, you must consider that the manipulated variable is sight versus some other sense or process, and the dependent variable, then, will be finding or not finding earthworms. Putting all of this into the problem statement would be unnecessarily cumbersome; it is all *implied* by the much simpler statement quoted, including the fact that this is a cause and effect relationship. Seeing causes finding.

17

of TV violence would consist of the number of the scenes so identified that was used in each case in the study (you could make an independent variable by showing one scene to some children, two to another group, etc.). You could define violence in children in terms of the number of times within a specified time span that a child damages, or makes a move that would ordinarily damage, a doll representing another person. These are operational definitions; they tell what you are going to do, observe, or measure with respect to the variable involved.

State your problem, then, in such a way that the variables identified in it are operationally defined.[4]

Identifying the Population or Conditions

In psychological, educational, or sociological experiments, it is the population in the human sense that is important. You need to define carefully the group to which you eventually want to generalize findings so that you can properly sample that population for the experiment. For example, if you want to generalize findings of a research study to physics teachers in the United States, you have defined the population — physics teachers in the United States. You are then bound to obtain a sample for your research that represents exactly that population. (Incidentally, this was done when the physical science study committee, PSSC, physics course was first developed, and a nationwide sample was randomly selected.)

In zoological studies the population will probably be a species, or other biological group, and again you must sample the group appropriately to be able to generalize findings to it.

In my ecological study, mentioned earlier, the population was "abandoned farmlands in southeastern Indiana." Rather than sampling, I used every abandoned field I could locate in the study; no doubt I missed some, but I was confident that at least I had an adequate sample, since I had tried to find *all* of the fields.

In chemical research, and physics too, you usually are not concerned with a population but rather with conditions. You can assume that barium chloride will behave the same way from one time to another *if* it is in the same conditions — same degree of purity, same solvent, same concentration, for example. You can assume that the momentum of a moving mass will be the same from time to time if it is measured under the same conditions — same mass, same effects of friction, same velocity, for example. In these cases, what

[4]True, operational definitions are not the only viable type. In some cases, but rather rarely, it might be acceptable to use a descriptive definition (the color of eyes will be determined by comparison with a five-color standard, blue, blue-green, green, hazel, brown) or, more rarely, a theoretical definition (atomic weight is defined as the mass in grams of a mole of atoms, expressed in atomic mass units rather than in grams), but notice that even these are operational to a considerable extent.

you should do in your problem statement, instead of specifying the population, is to specify the conditions. Sometimes this is called describing the *system* under investigation.

Stating the Problem in Historical or Descriptive Research

In descriptive research it may be difficult to state a problem in the terms suggested earlier. Commonly, the initial question in this kind of research is, "I wonder what ——— is like." (The popularity polls represent this type of research; the problem question is something like the following: What TV programs are most people watching at 8 PM? This is a way of asking, What is the viewing taste of the public like? Political polls also ask questions such as, Which candidate in this list would you vote for if you had to vote right now? This is a way of asking, What is the opinion of voters like?)

If you look carefully, you will see that there is really a relationship between variables in these problems, but one of the variables is the sample itself, which has to be *varied* in order to represent the population desired. It is stretching the point to admit this into the same categories of variable relationships as were discussed earlier. Why not just admit that descriptive research represents the need for a unique kind of problem statement, and this is, What is ——— like?

In historical research, of course, you are looking back into the records of events for your data, and so you have no chance to manipulate variables. Can you still state problems in terms of variable relationships? Sometimes you can, and sometimes you cannot. If your initial question is, I wonder what the events were that led to the Boer War, it will be difficult to state any variable relationships. It will be better simply to state the research problem, What were the events that led to the Boer War? But, note that you *can* express essentially the same question as a relationship between variables, and you would not be stretching very far to do so by asking, What was the *sequence* of events that led to the Boer War? You are then looking for historical events in relation to time, a *sequence* rather than just a listing. Doing this might make your research more valid because chances are pretty good that a given set of events, if they occurred in a different sequence, might lead to totally different results than those to which they actually did lead. In other words, time is likely to be an important factor in historical research.)

So, in historical research, too, you might need to state the problem factually, What were the events ——— ? You might also be able to state it in terms of variable relationships. Do the latter if you can. Use the following checklist to evaluate your research problems:

Is the problem stated as a *question* that needs to be answered?

Can data relevant to the question be obtained within a reasonable length of time and through reasonable procedures?

Can hypotheses be stated to guide the data collection?
Have operational definitions been used in the problem statement?
Are data collecting devices available? Or must new ones be prepared?
If a population is involved, does the researcher have access to it? Can an appropriate sample be obtained?
Does the nature of the question imply data analysis procedure?
Is the question worth answering (if answered, will it result in either new knowledge for the field or new applicability for existing knowledge)?

A PARADIGM FOR RESEARCH PLANNING

Now that you have a research problem defined, you can take a look at a general paradigm for research planning and see where you are in the process. The figure on page 21 presents the paradigm.

Notice that the paradigm suggests two alternate starting places for research, a need for information and a basic theory or conceptualization. The dotted lines connecting them suggest, however, that these are not mutually exclusive. Working with a basic theory might lead you to a need for some specific information that is not already available. Conversely, when you have identified a need for certain information, perhaps in connection with your job, you might begin the search for it by considering basic theories related to the area. The two starting places in the paradigm are meant to represent the fact that much, if not most, scientific and other so-called basic research commonly begins in theory, while most sociological and other so-called applied research commonly begins with a need for information.

I would like to make the point that neither of these types of research ought to be thought of as better than the other. Research is done for the purpose of establishing new knowledge, including finding new ways in which to manage knowledge that already exists. Who is to say that any given piece of new knowledge, or new technique, is more vital to the world than other pieces of knowledge? To the researcher, *his new knowledge* will always be the most important.

Having identified and stated your problem in research terms, you are now at the state research hypotheses point in the paradigm. It might be to your advantage to do what the paradigm suggests quite literally and write your research proposal formally to this point; in other words, write the literature search portion. If you decide to do this, skip the rest of this chapter for now and move to Chapter 3, Writing a Research Proposal.

STATING HYPOTHESES

Hypotheses come in four kinds, two of which are important in the written research proposal. The four categories are (1) underlying hypotheses, (2) re-

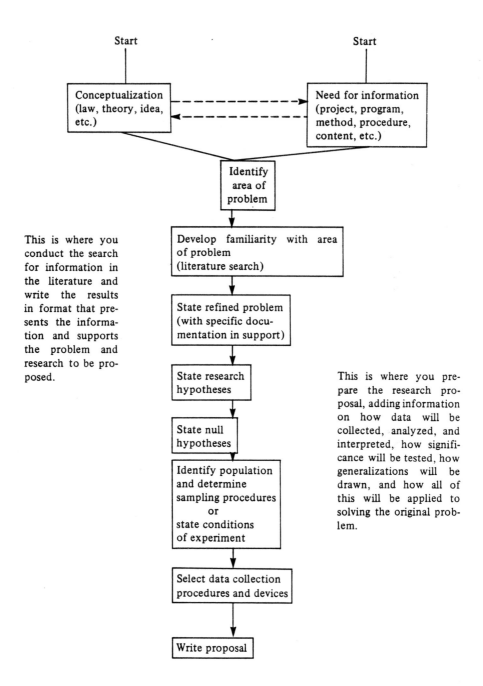

Start   Start

Conceptualization
(law, theory, idea,
etc.)

Need for information
(project, program,
method, procedure,
content, etc.)

Identify
area of
problem

This is where you
conduct the search
for information in
the literature and
write the results
in format that pre-
sents the informa-
tion and supports
the problem and
research to be pro-
posed.

Develop familiarity with area
of problem
(literature search)

State refined problem
(with specific docu-
mentation in support)

State research
hypotheses

State null
hypotheses

Identify population
and determine
sampling procedures
or
state conditions
of experiment

This is where you pre-
pare the research pro-
posal, adding information
on how data will be
collected, analyzed, and
interpreted, how signifi-
cance will be tested, how
generalizations will be
drawn, and how all of
this will be applied to
solving the original problem.

Select data collection
procedures and devices

Write proposal

search hypotheses, (3) null hypotheses, and (4) explanatory hypotheses.

An underlying hypothesis is the answer that you have in your mind to your initial question when you are beginning a research study. Suppose that your initial question was, I wonder if immunosuppressant drugs would have any positive effect on human patients in relief of the problems of diabetes mellitus.[5] No doubt you have an answer in your mind; the very reason you ask the question is probably that you have a conviction in your mind that the answer, in this case, is that the drugs do have such an effect.

An initial (underlying) hypothesis is usually of the "I'll bet you that ————" type. For example, I'll bet you that if I taught sixth graders English through the use of comic books and short stories they would end up reading more books on their own time than they would if I taught them with the regular English textbook; I'll bet you that if I did the right things to xenon it would form compounds; I'll bet you that the American Civil War was fought not because of the freeing of slaves but because of basic economic differences between sections of the country; etc.

The underlying hypothesis may not be directional, for example, I'll bet you that there will be observable differences between groups of students who are taught biology using dissections of preserved specimens and other groups taught through the use of overhead projections instead of dissections; I'll bet you that there is a relationship between teacher biases (as expressed by college professors) and student biases (as expressed by their students); etc.

If you can identify your underlying hypothesis, then the research hypothesis is just the result of expressing the underlying hypothesis in the terms described earlier in this chapter. Change the "I'll bet you ————" to a positive statement. "There will be ————." Using a previous statement, the research hypothesis would read, There will be differences between groups of students taught biology using dissections and groups using overhead projections instead of dissections.

Define your variables operationally, and put these definitions in the hypothesis statement: The average performance on (fill in test name) Standardized Achievement Test in Biology will be different for students in the ninth grade who have been taught through the use of dissections of preserved specimens of (fill in specimen names) and for students who have been taught the same content for the same length of time through the use of overhead projections instead of dissections.

See? You have a research hypothesis. Of course, it has a rather broad population, ninth grade biology students, but it does have the two variables operationally defined, and it does specify a relationship between

[5]Idea taken from "Progress Reported in Diabetes Research," *Chemical and Engineering News, 57:6*, 24 Dec. 1979.

them (the performance of one group will be different from that of the other) implying a cause-effect situation. The problem is not trivial; dissections in the classroom do cost money each year, while transparencies can be used over and over. You could actually carry out the research if you had access to biology classes. (Incidentally, you have specified two control variables in the hypothesis statement, the same content and the same length of time.) All you need to do to make the hypothesis still better is to be more specific in limiting the population, e.g. ninth gade biology students in San Antonio, Texas.

The preceding hypotheses could be expressed symbolically as follows:

Underlying hypothesis — Procedure A *is different in results*
from Procedure B

Research hypothesis — $\overline{X}_A = \overline{X}_B$

(The mean score on test X obtained by the group taught through method A is not equal to the mean score on test X obtained by the group taught through method B.)

Now if you wanted to express a directional research hypothesis it would be $\overline{X}_A > \overline{X}_B$. If your underlying hypothesis is directional for a reason, if you have some prior experience that leads you to believe that it is true, if you have found references in the literature that suggest that it is true, or if theory dictates that it ought to be true, then you must state your research hypothesis in directional fashion. This, in turn, dictates what you must do in any later statistical analysis.

A null hypothesis is simply the restatement of the research hypothesis in a form that says *no difference* will be found between the two groups or the hypothesized relationship between the two variables will not be found to exist. You can think of reasons for stating your hypothesis in null form: (1) this form indicates no bias on your part, you are merely interested in collecting data and finding out whether a relationship exists or not; (2) it does not sound as if you are out to "prove" something; (3) it will make results look better if you find only weak evidence against the null hypothesis; etc. But, the real reason for the null hypothesis has to do with the nature of "proof" in research. (Please see the section following the discussion of explanatory hypotheses for further explanation.)

After you have done your research and perhaps found that a hypothesized relationship does, indeed, exist between the variables you identified, your next question might well be, Why does it work this way? Why does tea with lemon dissolve polystyrene? (It actually does not, but *if it did* your question might be as indicated.) Why does teaching biology students in ninth grade seem to turn out better when you use real dissections, while with tenth grade students the use of overhead projections is better? Why do immunosuppressant drugs have a beneficial effect on patients with diabetes mellitus?

23

To answer such questions, you must resort to speculation; you must think about the situation and produce a *theory* that explains what was observed, or you may be able to use an existing theory for the explanation. In either case, what you decide upon as the explanation is still a hypothesis, beyond those used in your research, and it can be called an explanatory hypothesis.

It may be that this hypothesis, in turn, can serve as the starting place for further research. You might be able to test the hypothesis directly, or you might have to deduce predicted situations from it and test them. It may also be that this hypothesis cannot be tested experimentally. Theories would not remain theories if they could be experimentally tested and found to be correct, but then research rarely results in findings that are good "once and for all." (See the following section.)

"Proof" in Research

Since your research will usually be directed at finding cause and effect relationships, consider the following. If A is the cause of B, then whenever A is present B must always result, and whenever A is not present B must never result (assuming that A is the sole cause of B). The problems with proof hinge on those words always and never. Suppose in the diabetes problem you found that the drugs do indeed have beneficial effects on 89 percent of the cases treated. Does this percentage constitute proof that the hypothesized relationship is indeed there? It looks impressive, but what went wrong in the remaining cases?

Suppose that the average score of students taught biology by one method (as suggested in earlier hypotheses) was 85, and the average score of students taught by the competing method was 84; are the two results really different? If the scores were 86 and 83 would the results be different? 87 and 82? 88 and 81? What difference must be reached before you could conclude that the teaching method was the *cause* of a real difference?

These two cases should suggest that it will probably be impossible ever to say, "I have proven my research hypothesis," or, "I have disproven my null hypothesis." But, in the last quotation is the real reason for using a null hypothesis in much research. Suppose that in the world there is no correlation between the foot size and height of human beings; both characteristics are randomly distributed. There is a chance that you could locate just the right people for a sample in which you would find that the two characteristics are correlated. If you did this, you would conclude that the null hypothesis of no correlation must be rejected. But you would be making a mistake because of the way your sample was selected — it would not represent the world. Statistics have been worked out that will let you estimate the probability of finding such a correlated sample by random selection from a population in which there is no correlation. The probability gives you the chance occurrence of the relationship, and researchers have commonly agreed that they would seek a very low estimate of chance occurrence (commonly 5% or lower) before concluding that a relationship is "real."

In much research, proof will consist of rejecting the null hypothesis at some probability level, commonly .05. This means that the probability of finding the hypothesized relationship when the null hypothesis is actually correct (when there really is no relationship in the population) is five out of a hundred. You will not have *proven* the relationship, but you will have strong evidence that the null of the relationship is incorrect.

The same type of statistical reasoning may or may not be applicable in chemical and physical research. Much scientific theory is related to probability (for example, the location of an electron near a nucleus of an atom is represented by a cloud that is a depiction of the probability that the electron will be found in each given location), but it would be pretty hard to argue that if tea with lemon dissolves polystyrene one time it may not do so the next time you try it. If you observed such a phenomenon happening one time and not another, you would look for differences in the two systems, not for a probability that what happened was a chance occurrence.

I had better tell you now that the findings in the tea-with-lemon problem, interestingly, were that the polystyrene dissolves a component of the liquid, limonene, rather than the other way around. In the process, the polystyrene, of course, is changed in the area of solution, and a hole in the cup commonly results. This was found in the course of investigating the suspicion that the limonene dissolved polystyrene. Nuclear magnetic resonance spectra showed no polystyrene in the liquid after exposure; on the other hand, the cups showed a weight gain, according to a news report in *Chemical and Engineering News.*[6]

INTERLUDE IN PLANNING

Where are you now in planning your research? Check the paradigm again (Page 21). If you have completed a literature search in a problem and have come out of it with a research problem reasonably defined, if you have now stated that problem in the terms described earlier in this chapter, and if you have read the section on hypotheses, you are ready to *state* the hypotheses that will be used in your project and to go on from there. Think of the following list of questions and suggestions as a kind of worksheet to be followed in thinking through your project as you plan it.

[6]K.M. Reese, "New Findings in Lemon Tea Polystyrene Affair," (Newscripts column' *Chemical and Engineering News 58:*64, 14 Jan. 1980.

1. Have you identified a *problem area* in which you would like to find a specific problem that you could investigate in detail?
2. What research has already been done in the problem area? What *questions* have been answered (to your satisfaction), and what ones *remain to be solved*?
3. Do you have any *strong beliefs* regarding any of the unsolved problems in this area? Which of these beliefs are supported by (a) your own experiences, (b) evidence in research reports? Beliefs in the last category are the strongest for potential use in the next step in designing research.
4. Can you state an *underlying hypothesis* that you would like to investigate?
5. Which of the following is possible?
   a. Can you state the underlying hypothesis in research hypothesis form so that it can be tested?
   b. Does the underlying hypothesis suggest an alternate or related hypothesis that can be stated in research hypothesis form so that it can be tested?
   c. Can certain deductions that follow, if the underlying hypothesis is correct, be stated in research hypothesis form so that they can be tested?
6. Have you stated your research hypothesis so that (a) it states an expected relationship between two variables, (b) it describes the variables in operational terms, and (c) it defines a population?
7. Have you converted your research hypothesis into a null hypothesis statement indicating no difference between the variables? (This step is important if your research is with human subjects or if it is otherwise in an area where absolute findings are not to be expected.)
8. Did you find in your literature search any information that will be useful in any of the following areas: (a) sampling, (b) collecting data, (c) managing controls, (d) handling the treatment, (e) analyzing data, (f) interpreting findings, (g) drawing conclusions, or (h) publishing results)

THIS IS AS FAR AS THIS CHAPTER HAS GONE IN DESIGNING RESEARCH. Now you need to go on to new material on the rest of this worksheet.

9. How can you obtain a sample that represents the population which you defined in your research hypothesis? Is the population accessible? If not, what part of it is accessible? What size sample will you need for valid conclusions? How can you obtain this size sample? Must you obtain permission to collect data from the sample? If so, can this permission reasonably be expected to be granted, or had you better obtain permission before going further in your planning?

10. What type of data will be needed to test the hypotheses? Are instruments or devices available for collecting such data? Are they valid and reliable? Must you devise your own data collection procedures and devices, validate them and establish reliability? If the data will be historical or descriptive, do you have access to the sources that will be needed?

11. How will the data be analyzed? Will the data be numerical, or can they be quantized? Will data be in "count" form; if so what does a number mean? What statistics will best test the null hypothesis in your case? Do you have calculation skills for the needed statistics, or do you have access to a consultant? Is a computer and program needed? If so, is it available to you? If data will not be numerical, what methods of tabulation or other visual display can be used?

12. What is the nature of the decision you ultimately want to make? Will a decision be such that it could result in (a) large expense, (b) danger to human life, or (c) labeling individuals with possible resulting psychological effects? Or, will the decision result in more innocuous eventualities? In light of these consequences, what significance level will you use in interpreting findings?

13. In what ways must you compromise between an ideal research design for this study and what is possible to you? Have you already made all possible compromises?

14. Will your research be internally valid; will it have both external population validity and external ecological validity? (Go back to items 9 and 10 and consider whether you have built in adequate controls, whether you have pretesting or other means of assuring that the treatment is indeed the cause of observed changes, that you have thought of all applicable variables, and that your sample will indeed represent the population to which you want to generalize.)

15. Is it possible to publish your research findings? (Publication need not be widespread, but research that only you know about will not be very useful as new knowledge to the world.)

Among questions 9 through 15, guidelines or assistance can be readily found in textbooks in research methods if needed. The only area to be explained in this book will be setting the significance level.

SETTING SIGNIFICANCE LEVELS

It was hinted in item 12 of the previous section that certain kinds of conclusions from research might be more "drastic" than others. If you found a new cure for some disease, drug companies would "tool up" to produce the materials, doctors would have to learn new techniques, and the whole discovery would be very expensive overall. If you discovered that a new method of teaching reading was much more effective than the old process for students in your school system, the results might or might not be expensive. If it meant that new books had to be bought for all schools and that teachers had to be retrained in their use, it might be expensive, but if all that was required was that the teachers behave in a different way or present materials in a different sequence, the results might not be expensive at all.

Another kind of expense to consider is the effect on human lives. All new treatments for diseases must be carefully checked for undesirable side effects before they are put into general use. Any psychological effects of testing individuals need to be carefully considered; any labeling that could result in damage to the self-concept of individuals must be carefully avoided. Certainly anything that is life threatening must be avoided in research. (There are obvious exceptions, even to this last statement; you will read about prisoners with life sentences volunteering as subjects in life-threatening experiments, for example.) ''Expensive'' is used to refer to any of these situations.

If the results of research are likely to be expensive, you should be very conservative in setting significance levels. What you would like to achieve in your research is to *reject the null hypothesis*. Rejecting the null hypothesis means that the research hypothesis is acceptable, and this is what you really hope to find. You set a rejection level for the null hypothesis, perhaps .05, which is the standard level, and then if your statistic's value reaches this level or exceeds it, you reject the null hypothesis. Actually, .05 is a low rejection level. Using it means that you run the risk of rejecting the null hypothesis when you should not (when it is, in fact, true) only five times out of a hundred. But you *do* have the possibility that the null hypothesis will, in fact, be correct those five times out of a hundred. In a very expensive result situation, this might not be acceptable.

In the case of someone's recommending that saccharin be taken off the food market because it was a possible cause of cancer, this was a very expensive result of research. The null hypothesis in this example would have been that there was no relationship between saccharin and cancer in human beings. The research was carried out with mice as the test organism. Two kinds of cost had to be considered. If, indeed, a relationship was found between the two variables and saccharin was to be removed from the market, many, many foods would have to be changed, many companies would have to spend large amounts of money making these changes, many people would object because they wanted to remain on sugar-free diets, etc. This would involve a large expense in money. On the other hand, if there were even a pretty good possibility that there was a relationship between the two variables, it would be smart to prevent the use of a food that could possibly be harmful and in doing this to save many lives. The first argument would suggest that the researchers should be very conservative in setting rejection levels for the null hypothesis, while the second would suggest very liberal rejection levels. To save the large amounts of money involved in the first case, the researcher might set rejection levels at .001 (only 1 out of 1,000 chances to make an error), which is very conservative. But, to be careful and possibly save lives, the researcher might set rejection levels at .25 (25 times out of 100 he would have made an error), which is very liberal.

Do you see the reasoning? If rejecting the null hypothesis will be expensive, what you should do is make it hard for you to reject the null hypothesis. This means that you would set the rejection, or significance, level at a low figure, less than .05 perhaps in the .01, .001, or even .0001 area. At these levels you will not reject many null hypotheses, but you also will not *mistakenly* reject them. Conversely, if the results are not likely to be expensive, what you might well do is make it easy to reject the null hypothesis. After all, at the .25 level of significance you still have only 25 chances out of 100 of making a mistake, and the remaining 75 out of 100 positive chances are not bad.

This discussion has been about making Type I errors, rejecting the null hypothesis when it is in fact correct. A Type II error is failing to reject the null hypothesis when it is in fact wrong and *should* be rejected. This is related to what is called the *power of the test of significance*. You may want to consult another reference regarding the power of a test if your concern is making a Type II error.

CHAPTER 3

WRITING A RESEARCH PROPOSAL

Y ou are writing a research proposal for a specific audience; never lose sight of this group or individual as you try to follow the guidelines given here. If your proposal is to be submitted to a funding agency, guidelines will be provided by that agency, and you must follow these for your efforts to be considered. If your proposal is for a thesis or dissertation, your audience consists of at least two segments; you must satisfy your supervisory committee that what you want to do is worthwhile and appropriate, and you must convince a supervising administrator (usually a college dean or a graduate school dean) that what you want to do will be worth the credit allowed for a thesis or dissertation. (If, by any chance, your proposal is to meet a course requirement, then you must satisfy the professor that you know what you are doing and that you know how to write a proposal correctly. No doubt, the professor will have provided some guidelines as to what is acceptable.) This chapter will help you write the proposal, but you must be careful to put it into the format required by your particular situation.

The commonly required parts of a proposal for funding are as follows:
Title and cover
Abstract, clearly outlining the problem and procedures
Problem statement, with justification
Literature search, primary emphasis on (a) justification for the problem and (b) techniques for solution
Design
   Population and sampling (controls)
   or
   Conditions of experiment (treatment)
   Methods of data collection (place the instruments in an appendix)
   Methods of data analysis
Procedures for solving the problem
Time schedule
Budget (including personnel required)
The general format for a thesis or dissertation, however, is the following:
Approval form, title, and cover

Abstract, outlining primarily the problem and procedures, but also showing
potential applications
Problem statement
Literature search
Design
    Population and sampling (controls)
    or
    Conditions of experiment (treatment)
    Methods of data collection
    Methods of data analysis
Plans for completion
    Registrations
    Timing
    Personnel
    Writing plans for final paper

The major differences in format are that the academic paper will require
approvals (although the other may also) and the funding paper will require
careful documentation of need and a detailed budget and time schedule for the
work to be done.

STATING THE PROBLEM

In the proposal you have the choice of first stating the problem area, with
which you began the literature search, and then defining the precise problem
later or of stating the research problem at the very beginning. Except for explaining your reasoning processes, there is little need to state the problem area
first. Perhaps the major reason for doing so would be to show how your research problem fits into a larger problem that may be of broader importance.

State the research problem right away. You may not want to begin the very
first sentence with, "The problem to be investigated in this study will be . .
.," but you should insert this kind of statement in the first paragraph at least.
At the beginning of the proposal you do not need to explain the problem in the
full operational definition terminology described in an earlier chapter; your
purpose here is merely to introduce the problem to the reader, not to define it
thoroughly for him. An example of a possible first paragraph follows.

    Today, because X-rated movies and "adult" bookstores are available to anyone
who wants to visit them and because newspapers are filled daily with reports of ag-
gravated assault and forcible rape, it is easy to suspect that there might be a cause and
effect relationship between pornography and violence. Indeed, several years ago a
commission on obscenity and pornography was appointed by President Nixon to
investigate whether such a cause-effect relationship did exist, and the commission
reported no evidence that this was the case. This was a long time ago, however, and
the number of violent crimes reported daily has been increasing at an alarming rate,
according to FBI reports, in the last two years. The question to be investigated in the

study proposed here will be, "Is there now a correlation between the prevalence of pornographic materials, which are accessible to nearly all, and the rate of increase in reported violent crimes?" The question will be investigated using data already in existence and adding to it data that has accumulated since earlier studies were done. If a correlation is established, then information will be sought, in a later study, regarding the possibility of a cause and effect relationship.

Notice that the problem of the study is stated in the first paragraph, but it is not stated in precise terms. Notice also that the stage is set for a second study if the first one produces the expected results. A beginning paragraph like this one would then be followed up with explanatory materials regarding the general nature of the study to be done and some indication of how the author (the researcher) intends to solve the problem at the end. (Remember that this has been preceded by an abstract, which should be done in the way those discussed earlier in this book were done.)

WRITING THE LITERATURE SEARCH REPORT

You should have three kinds of notes, which you took while you were doing the literature search: (1) abstracts of research reports, (2) factual information taken from books or other sources, and (3) statements of opinion presented by authors whose materials you read. Furthermore, your abstracts should be indexed with code symbols so that you can tell at a glance what kind of information is in each of them. Sort these out now.

Determine where you want your literature search report to go. What do you want it to tell the reader? To what question or questions do you want it to point? How much do you want it to contribute toward (1) justifying the study, (2) explaining the procedures to be used in the study, (3) providing actual information related to your problem, (4) doing something else?

Organize the research abstracts, physically rearrange them, so that their contents tell the story on which you have decided. The following order is suggested (assuming that all of these are of importance in your case):

1. Abstracts that justify your study
2. Abstracts that help to divide the problem area into subproblems
3. Abstracts that provide information indicating that certain of these subproblems have been solved
4. Abstracts that lead to a given subproblem (yours) that still remains to be solved
5. Abstracts that provide definition of your precise problem
6. Abstracts that provide any background information on your precise problem that might be applicable in carrying out your research
7. Abstracts that suggest data collection procedures, analytical tools, instruments, or other devices that you intend to use in your research

Next, organize the rest of your notes so that they fit into the pattern already established, so that they contribute to the story line. (Most of the opinion notes will probably fit into the justification section, for example.) Read through all of the notes in the sequence in which you have organized them. This will give you an indication of two things: (1) how well the set of materials tells the story you want it to tell and (2) what interspersed material you will have to add, i.e. your own comments, evaluations, summaries, and connecting paragraphs to make the whole set read smoothly.

You are finally ready to write the literature search report. Do not simply use the abstracts as you initially wrote them in your notes but, rather, describe each of them in smooth flowing paragraph form. *Do* include, however, all of the information that was in the original abstract, unless there are some items that are obviously extraneous to the point you are trying to make. Do not quote very often; use paraphrasing instead. Avoid stereotypical repetition of terminology from one study to the next; write with a bit of style, using alternate terms and phrases (you do not want your readers to become bored).

When you encounter several parallel studies, or some that seem to make the same points, describe one of them in detail and cite the rest to support the first. Summarize throughout the writing, whenever you come to the end of a major section. Summarize at the end of the literature search also, and be sure that you restate the problem in this summary.

Throughout the writing you must, of course, provide citations to the literature you are using. If no format has been specified for citations, the general rule is consistency — you must use the same format throughout the paper. The format recommended, if there is no other format specified, is that of the American Psychological Association (APA). Get an APA *Publication Manual* or check journal articles for this format.

Be sure that you have a complete bibliography of the articles, books, and other sources used in this section, as well as those to be used in any other part of the proposal.

The research proposal is a formal document and, as such, must (1) never contain any levity, (2) be typed error free, and (3) be written in an impersonal style, or passive voice ("The data will be collected . . ." rather than "I will collect data . . ."). If you must refer to yourself, you are, in third person, "the author" or "the investigator." If there is ever any doubt about what a phrase such as "this study" might refer to say "the study here proposed" when refering to your own research and "the study by . . ." when referring to another project.

I have to insert a personal note at this point. Many, I suspect most, graduate students have grown up with the impression that when you write a paper in which you cite literature sources you are supposed to take statements from the sources or conclusions from them and use these in support of your own ideas. Thus, a paper would consist mostly of your own statements of ideas with citations only briefly lifted from the literature. This is not the case with a research literature search report. This report must contain the bulk of each study cited so that the reader will be able to judge whether or not it really does what you say it does with respect to your study. You must change your way of writing and do a lot more paraphrasing and a lot less stating of your own ideas in this paper than you are probably used to. Ninety percent of the paper should consist of descriptions of the work of others. Go back and check; maybe you put too much of yourself into this report.

DESCRIBING THE DESIGN

Since you have already decided on your population (if yours is the kind of study that requires a population) in connection with stating your research problem, the design may already be fixed. If not, you now have to decide how you will carry out the research. Your basic choices are the following:

1. Historical research
2. Descriptive research, dealing with the status quo
3. Correlational or predictive research
4. Ex post facto cause-effect research, sometimes called causal-comparative research
5. Longitudinal research, sometimes called follow-up studies
6. Trend-seeking research (this includes the use of case studies and any other data-collecting techniques in which the purpose is actually prediction rather than description)
7. Experimental research in which one or more variables are manipulated in order to seek cause-effect relationships
8. Experimental research in which a theory is used to make some prediction, which is then tested

These basic designs have more to do with how you will obtain data than with anything else. You should not, for example, decide that you want to do longitudinal research because you like to keep records and follow up on events; you should make this decision because that is the best way for you to obtain the data needed to solve the problem you have identified.

A brief description of how data is collected in each type of research follows.

Historical Research

The data in this type of research comes from historical records. It is likely to be verbal, although there certainly are instances in which numerical data can be utilized. (These more commonly fit under causal-comparative research, however.) The primary validity problem that the researcher has to deal with is whether or not the historical records can be believed. The solutions to this problem are as follows: (1) use primary sources, e.g. eyewitness accounts, minutes of meetings, etc., as often as possible, use secondary sources, e.g. newspaper accounts not written by an eyewitness reporter, historians' summaries, etc., only when necessary; (2) with either type of source, use both internal and external critical analysis to check on truthfulness. Internal criticism checks on whether or not the account has internal agreement. Are there any contradictions within the account? Does it "make sense?" External criticism checks on the agreement of the account with other historical accounts of the same time period.

Status Quo Descriptive Research

The popular opinion surveys, the television and radio program rating studies, the political polls are examples of descriptive research. The data is collected by examining the status quo, and the results are a description of the status quo. The data collection devices are commonly checklists, questionnaires, and interview guides. The use of panels of experts is common, as is the Q-sort technique, in getting some sort of quantification of the data.

A good friend of mine used to do this type of research all the time. He thought the existing situation should be described in careful terms before attempting to do any kind of experimental research that would tamper with parts of the situation, and so he did many surveys that resulted in descriptions of the status quo. He was able to get grants to support this research. He convinced funding agencies also that the status quo needed to be described. Do not put down descriptive research; it *is* valuable, and at least this friend of mine had fun doing it.

Correlational or Predictive Research

You almost certainly must have numerical data to do correlational or predictive research. If your data is verbal, you should think of the study as a trend-seeking investigation instead of a correlational one. If the data will be analyzed by calculating correlation coefficients or constructing multiple correlation matrices or multiple regression graphs, the study is surely seeking to make predictions of one variable from a knowledge of one or more other variables. An example of this is the one suggested earlier, the relationship between the availability of pornographic materials to the public and the records of the incidence of violent crimes. As this example suggests, you may or may not be interested in establishing a cause and effect relationship between the two variables also; if your purpose is initially to seek a correlation between them, then the study is a correlational one.

Ex Post Facto Cause-Effect Research

Ex post facto cause-effect research is a very specific type of research in which you have an existing situation whose historical causes you want to establish. Because you will not be able to manipulate those cause variables, you will never be very sure that a cause and effect relationship has been established, but you can certainly obtain the kind of evidence that will convince others. Suppose, for example, that you wanted to find the causes behind some communities' having high incidences of cancer and others' having low incidences. Your present data would consist of the incidences themselves, which can be compared statistically to determine whether or not they are significantly unlike, and the individual cases of persons who have had cancer in each community. You would next search for some theory that would provide a clue to possible causes of the difference between communities — for example, you might think of differences in genetic patterns among closely related families, you might think about differences in the regular water or food utilized in the communities, or you might wonder about work patterns (Do most people in one community work in a certain factory?) or perhaps about the very soil underlying each community (remember the Love Canal).

With a theory, or theories, in mind you would examine the records and past conditions of each community, searching for the usual cause-effect situation (if cause is present, effect is always observed; if cause is absent, effect is never observed). So, your data would consist of a record of whatever historical events your theory had suggested as possible causes; it might be numerical, it might be descriptive, it might be almost any kind of data.

Longitudinal Research

My master's thesis research, which I described earlier, was definitely longitudinal research. What I was trying to do was to find a sequence of events (actually of plant communities) that might be expected to occur on abandoned fields. As I said in the thesis, the most logical way to do the research would have been to find a field that was just abandoned and observe it yearly for up to 100 years. This way I would have been absolutely certain of the sequence of plant communities on that particular field — but I would never have gotten the thesis finished. What I did, of course, was to locate many abandoned fields, each being abandoned for a different length of time, and observe the plant communities on them. Then, I inferred that the succession on an individual field would be the same as the composite picture. What resulted was a cross-sectional study, but this does not change the nature of the research; it was still longitudinal because of the nature of the question I was trying to answer, and I was able to complete the thesis.

As with correlational or predictive research, the data in longitudinal research might be in almost any form. The key to the type of research done is, as was indicated previously, in the question. If the question asks for a series of events to be identified, the research is follow-up research.

Trend-seeking Research

Trend-seeking research is predictive, of course. The big difference between this category and correlational research, described earlier, is that there you intended to make calculations of correlation coefficients, or something like them, whereas in seeking trends you are looking for any kind of trend (usually seen in a table, in a verbal sequence, or at best in a pictorial graph) that will enable you to predict future events. The data will ordinarily not be numerical.

This type of research is commonly tied either with historical data collection or with descriptive surveys. It could even be related to ex post facto research, if your goal is to establish the trends as causes rather than only as predictors.

Experimental, Variable Manipulation, Research

Experimental research covers the whole set of research designs in which the goal is to find cause and effect relationships. These designs are common in educational research or research in other behavioral sciences, and if this is your area (and if you need help) you should read a book by Campbell and Stanley outlining these designs in detail.[1]

Experimental Research, Theory Based

Theory-based experimental research covers the whole range of usually scientific research, although it can certainly apply in other fields also, in which the basic procedure is to produce a theory that would give you a clue to the solution for your problem; use the theory to predict an event or events, and then set up whatever systems need to be manipulated to see if the prediction comes true. Indeed, the research is sometimes done simply to test the theory, rather than to find the answer to some more prosaic question. In such cases it would probably be considered to be basic research — as opposed to applied research. You might call this the try-it-and-see design, since what you do is predict that something ought to be observed under given circumstances; then you set up the circumstances (try it) and observe whether or not what you expected happens (and see).

WRITING THE ELEMENTS OF YOUR RESEARCH DESIGN

Name your design, then describe what you intend to do within the basic format. Your explanation should include all of the following that fit what you intend to do.

[1] D.T. Campbell, Julian C. Stanley, *Experimental and Quasi-Experimental Designs for Research* (Chicago, Rand McNally & Co., 1963). This is also Chapter V in N. Gage, ed., *Handbook of Research on Teaching* (American Educational Research Association, 1963).

Population and Sampling

Any experiment in which you want to generalize beyond the sample actually used in the research requires the identification of a population. Probably the only experiments excluded are some in theory-based experimental research which are related to chemical or physical systems. If yours is the type of experiment in which population must be identified, you already know what this population is; however, you must restate it in the design section of your proposal. Then you must tell how you intend to obtain a representative sample of that population.

Some general rules follow. (1) You should obtain the largest sample possible; the larger the sample, the more likely your research is to have valid applications. (2) In the absence of other guidelines, as a rule you should take not less than 10 percent of the population as your sample. (3) As another rule, you should have at least thirty cases in research with human subjects; statistical tables suggest that many values have "break points" or converge around this size. (4) For surveys and other cases where representative sampling is preferable to random sampling, make sure that all subgroups are represented; this usually means a much larger total sample than in other studies. (5) A large sample is also required if you are unable to control certain variables, if you have reason to expect that only small differences will show up between groups, and if you are not sure of the reliability of your measuring devices. In the last case you will have to establish reliability of the instrument simultaneously with using it to measure the variable, and you will need more subjects.

Two specific rules are as follows:

1. For correlational studies simply decide upon the desired significance level (perhaps .05) and the desired correlation coefficient (in order to be able to use it in prediction, maybe .70 or above). Then look in a table showing significance of correlation coefficients in relation to degrees of freedom. Add 2 and you have the minimum sample size. (For p = .05 and r = .70 the minimum sample size would be 8 subjects.) Then make sure that you have a sample larger than this for your study.

2. In two-group comparison cases where some sort of test or numerical measure is going to be utilized for the dependent variable, use the following formula to estimate the minimum number of subjects needed in each group.[2]

$$N = \frac{2s^2 \times t^2}{D^2}$$

[2]W.R. Borg, M.D. Gall, *Educational Research, An Introduction,* 3rd ed. (New York, Longman Inc., 1979), p. 200.

s is the expected standard deviation of scores on the measuring device, t is the value of the t test needed for signifiance, and D is the estimated value of the difference to be found between the two groups.

Describe in your research proposal both how you intend to obtain a sample and why you chose the size sample specified.

Conditions of Experiment

In those studies where population and sampling are not required parts, but possibly in other studies as well, you need to describe the conditions of the experiment. If it is to involve a chemical or physical system, identify the components, state concentrations to be studied or used, specify conditions of mixing or purifying, describe containers and other apparatus, etc.

Recent reports (at the time of writing this book) have appeared indicating that it has been found possible to place a gene for the production of human leukocyte interferon into a bacterium, which will then produce a couple of interferon molecules. This is a vital step in the progress of examining possible cancer treatments, since interferon is horribly expensive, and less expensive ways of producing it would make it more readily available for what promises to be potentially valuable research. Suppose that you were trying to write a research proposal related to the studies that produced this finding. What you would specify as "conditions of the experiment" might include such things as (1) the bacterium to be used, or possibly several to be tried, (2) culturing techniques before and after injecting the gene, (3) temperature, pressure, atmosphere — whatever of this nature you consider important in the experiments, (4) apparatus to be used in "injecting" the gene, its treatment and use, (5) measuring devices to be used to determine results, and so on. You can readily see that any agency funding research would want to know that you had made your plans carefully and that you knew what you were doing. Descriptions of the conditions of an experiment such as this would help in such explanations.

Controls

Long ago researchers were advised to follow the "Law of the Only Significant Variable." This meant that you must have only one independent variable (or predictor variable in correlational research) at one time; that is, only one variable should be manipulated in a given piece of research. Since the invention of analysis of variance techniques, however, it has been possible to discover interaction effects, sometimes the most important findings in a study, when two or more variables are treated as independent variables simulataneously. Nevertheless, whatever variables might have important effects as causes in an experiment and are not going to be measured must be controlled in some way. If intelligence, for example, is important in learning studies and if you design a study in which you will measure the effects of a given teaching strategy on the learning (achievement) of students, then you must control intelligence. But, your proposal must tell (1) what variables you consider it necessary to control, possibly explaining why and (2) how you intend to manage the controls.

Treatment

In the treatment section you should describe in detail the manner in which the independent variable(s) will be manipulated. Timing is important. (When will treatment begin and end?) Length of time within the treatment is important. (How long per day will the treatment be applied?) It is important to know who will do the manipulation. In a teaching experiment, for example, it could be vital that the same teacher be used for both experimental and control groups, or it could be that this is exactly the wrong thing to do; you must explain your procedures. What is the setting in which the treatment will occur? Have extraneous conditions that might effect the outcome of the experiment been controlled?

Please see later sections in this book if you need specific guidance in planning your treatment or the manipulation of variables.

Methods of Data Collection

Data collection procedures can be classified into three types: (1) automatic procedures where a machine of some kind records information, (2) semiautomatic procedures where some instrument such as a test is used as the information-collecting device, but the actual recording of information depends upon the interpretation of the instrument (scoring the test) by a human being, and (3) subjective procedures where interpretation and recording are easily confounded. An example of the last point might be the recording of classroom observation data in an educational experiment. Another might be the recording of personal observations by a biological researcher growing plants under different conditions and noting daily appearance.

Since your major concern with data, in addition to getting *usable* information, is that it be correct, you must give thought in planning research to the validity and reliability of the devices for collecting data. Some possible ways of ensuring both of these in each type of data collection follow.

AUTOMATIC DATA COLLECTION PROCEDURES

Much astronomical research data is collected by automatic cameras; a lot of chemical data is collected by electronic recording devices connected to such instruments as pH meters, diffraction apparatus, electrical conduction meters, and much more sophisticated devices; some psychological data is collected by automatic measuring devices and recorded mechanically, and the same is true of much medical information needed in research.

With automatic data collection, you have little concern over reliability; the devices will give you the same information from one time to another, and it will be subject only to the variations allowed by uncertainty in the measuring device used.

Validity is another question, however. Whether or not the physiological changes measured and recorded by a "lie detector" can be equated with truthfulness is a validity question, for example. The instruments are reliable; they will give the same results every time but their validity is subject to human judgment. Unfortunately, this is *always* true, every question of validity is ultimately settled by dependence on human judgment. You see, the question of validity is, "Does this device measure what it is said to measure?" If the device in question is, for example, a recording balance, there is not really very much doubt that what is being measured is comparative mass. (Even in this case, however, judgment enters into the picture in that someone had to standardize or calibrate the instrument originally.)

Suppose, however, that the instrument used is a nuclear magnetic resonance (NMR) spectrometer and that the situation is the study of the relationship between tea with lemon and polystyrene.[3] If the NMR spectrum is supposed to show the amount of dissolved polystyrene (actually, you will remember, limonene dissolves in polystyrene), you must certainly do something to establish a relationship between NMR output and actual, i.e. known, amounts of dissolved polystyrene. This process, of course, is the one involved in establishing validity. What you do is demonstrate with a known material that the device to be used does indeed record what you already know to be the case. You may want to demonstrate this, not once, but several times, and then you have a strong argument that the device is valid for the intended purpose.

So, with any automatic data recording device, what you need to do is to demonstrate that it does indeed record the variations known to exist in a situation, and then you can argue that it will also do so in an unknown situation. (See the following section, however, for an additional problem.)

SEMIAUTOMATIC DATA COLLECTION PROCEDURES

The data in most educational research is collected through the use of tests of some kind, achievement tests, intelligence tests, measures of self-concept, measures of reading level, etc. Also, in much survey research, data is col-

---

[3]NMR was actually used in connection with this problem. K.M. Reese, "New Findings in Lemon Tea Polystyrene Affair," (Newscripts column) *Chemical and Engineering News*, 58:64, 14 Jan. 1980.

lected through use of questionnaires or interview guides or checklists. All of these are semiautomatic in that the nature of the data is specified by the device used (so that it will be uniform across subjects), but the scoring of the device and the recording of data may depend on interpretation made by a human being.

With tests, both validity and reliability are questionable. A written test may or may not yield the same results from one time to another. You know yourself that you could take a test on one day when you felt fine and alert and make a good score on it, but on another day when you were ill or preoccupied with other cares you might score quite a bit lower on the same test. If a test does not repeatedly measure a variable in the same way, it is not reliable.

Tests also have the problem of validity; does the test measure what it is said to measure? Unfortunately, it is not as easy with a test to demonstrate that it is valid by using a "known" situation because you cannot know the "known" either. Consider that if you were trying to validate a new intelligence test you might do so by comparing its readings when it is taken by persons whose intelligence is known. But, how do you know the intelligence of an individual? You can do so only through the use of another "intelligence test." That test had to be validated too. From this it is easy to see that validity ultimately goes back to a time when someone had to say, "This test does measure what it says it measures."

This is where another validity problem develops. When the variable that is being measured is a physical one, length, mass, volume, etc., there is really not too much doubt that it is indeed being measured by a given device (when the demonstration with knowns is made as described previously). But, when the variable is a conceptual one, or, as it is often called, a *construct* (a variable that has, in effect, been invented to explain phenomena), how can you ever know that you are measuring it? Can you actually measure "creativity" or "respect" or other such abstract variables?

What you must do in such cases, since you do have to deal with the validity of measurements when you are writing your research proposal, is to (1) utilize the idea of operational definitions (so that the test you want to use is *defined* as a measure of the variable or, rather, the variable is defined in terms of the results with this specific test) and (2) convince your readers that your operational definition is a proper one. A good way to effect such convincing is to demonstrate that others have used the same operational definition. This, in effect, is what you do when you establish validity of a new test by comparing its results with those given by an older test that is presumed to measure the same variable; the older test has been defined as a measure of the variable (by someone else), and you are using it as your standard for comparison.

In writing your research proposal, you must tell the readers either what the validity and reliability of your measuring devices are or how you intend, within the research project, to establish validity and reliability of the measuring devices.

In one of my research studies, I wanted to use a standardized test of achievement in high school chemistry, so I picked what I assumed would be a valid and reliable test, a published and widely used one (whose name I will not divulge here). In the proposal I simply indicated this fact, and it was accepted by the proposal readers, and the research was funded. However, when I inquired into the original validating and reliability-establishing procedures, I was not satisfied at all that these had been adequately carried out. Validity was really not much of a problem, since it is not too difficult to establish *content* validity in a subject like chemistry (by the old "jury" technique). But, to deal with reliability I took much of the original data (not my data) for the test and re-established standards, which then became the operational definition of "achievement in chemistry." Then my data were compared to these standards, using the same test.

DATA COLLECTION BY SUBJECTIVE PROCEDURES

Any kind of observational data will be subjective, since it depends on the interpretation placed on what is seen by the observer. (As was indicated earlier, interpretation and recording can be confounded. For example, an observer standing on the sidewalk sees a woman run by a window in a nearby house. Then, immediately he sees a man run by the window with a broom raised over his head as if to strike. What he records, for the police whom he calls, is that the man was chasing the woman intending to strike her with the broom. As soon as the words "intending to strike" were inserted here, there was an interaction of actual data and interpretation, that is, this is the observer's thought. What might really have been happening is that the woman was running from a mouse and the man was chasing the mouse with the broom.) If this is the kind of data on which you will have to depend in your research, you must explain in your proposal how you are going to make it as valid and reliable as possible, how you are going to get around the subjectiveness. Some possibilities are as follows.

1. Quantifying

If at all possible, you should plan to quantify observational data; you can analyze numbers, even if they are not very meaningful, where it is very difficult to analyze words. If you can count responses by categories, you will have data that can be handled better than if you just record responses. If you can set up a questionnnaire in such a way that the numbers of "yes" and "no" responses can be counted for each item, you can analyze the results. If you can construct an instrument so that the person using it indicates agreement or disagreement with statements (a Likert type of scale) you will be able to get "scores" that can be handled.

One of the best inventions for quantifying observer data on school classrooms (indeed, on any group interaction situation) is the Flanders' interaction analysis procedure.[4]

What this procedure does basically is to enable the observer to check off the type of behavior that is being observed each three seconds (the original interaction analysis instrument had ten categories of behavior, and it took a bit of training to become adept at checking one of them each three seconds) or whatever other time period is appropriate. The time is short so that the observer cannot really stop to think, to interact with the data, but must simply record what is happening. Since the intervals are regular, the resulting data can be interpreted in percentage of time each type of action was observed — the data has been quantified.

You might be able to locate, or invent, other devices for quantifying data, but quantify if at all possible.

2. Repeating Observations

The simplest way of repeating observations is to have two or more observers present, each independently recording what he sees. Of course, just having observations repeated does not avoid the interpretation-recording interaction problem. What you must do is establish interobserver reliability. If the data is verbal, you can do this by comparing the observations; the extent to which they agree tells you whether or not the two (or more) observers can be relied upon to report the same data from any given situation. If the data can also be quantified, you can calcuate, by correlation techniques interobserver reliability and report it more precisely.

What is commonly done is to have the several observers who are to collect data in a research project make observations on a number of situations. Then their observations are compared as described previously and discussed so that each can see how he is making his observations differently from others. Then all agree on how they will make each kind of observation expected. Finally, all observe another set of situations to see if they are now in closer agreement than they were before. This is repeated until agreement is as close as is desired for the study, then the real data collection begins. Repeatedly during the real data collection, the observers are checked to make sure that they are still in agreement, that the interobserver reliability is still high.

3. Recording the Whole Situation

Either audio – or videotape can be used to record situations, rather than having live observers present. Of course, the situations will still have to be "observed" or translated into data to be used in the research, but once the situations have been recorded, you can, at your leisure, apply the preceding

[4]Ned A. Flanders, *Analyzing Teaching Behavior.* (Boston, Addison-Wesley, 1970).

techniques. Recording has the additional advantage that an observer can determine interobserver reliability with himself. He can observe a situation and then, some time later, observe it again to see if he still sees the same things in the same way.

The disadvantage of recording is expense. You might think either that having live observers present or that having recording equipment in a room would have some effect on the behavior of subjects. This is true, but there is no way to say which is worse. Furthermore, if you simply do not use the data recorded the first two or three times with either observers or recording equipment, subjects quickly get used to their presence and return to natural behavior.

Whichever of the previous procedures fit into your plans should be described in detail in your research proposal. The basic organization (at least the basic way of thinking through this section) should be as follows: (1) What kind of data is dictated by the problem stated? What kind of information is needed to solve the problem or test the hypothesis? (2) What devices are needed to collect this information? Are they available or must they be developed? (3) How will the data actually be obtained? Who, when, where, with what subjects, etc.? (4) How will the validity and reliability of the data be established? Are the devices valid and reliable or will these have to be established as part of the research project? If the latter is the case, how will these be done? (5) How much data will be needed? How long should observations be continued? When should testing occur? (6) What limitations will the data have? How must conclusions be modified (or cautiously stated) by limitations? Can any of the limitations be overcome in this study or must they be accepted?

Methods of Data Analysis

The readers of your research proposal will probably be willing to assume that if data is properly acquired it can be analyzed and interpreted, either by you or with the help of consultants. If your proposal is for a thesis or dissertation, however, you may find that this section is one of the most important. In any case, the very least that you should include in this section of the proposal is an indication of how you will obtain the necessary help to get the data analyzed.

Describe the statistics to be used, if appropriate. If a computer program is to be utilized, identify it or its source, and be sure to include computer time in your budget. If consultants are needed, you should identify them in advance and name them in the proposal. Again, you may need to include consultant fees in the budget. It may be necessary to justify a given type of analysis. For example, if you plan to do a nonparametric analysis of data, you may have to explain why such techniques are preferable to more powerful parametric procedures.

Tell what you intend to do about significance levels. If you are going to set them in advance, state the levels here in the proposal. If levels are other than standard, tell why you chose them. If you are not going to state levels in advance, tell why and also tell how you plan to interpret findings in significance terms.

If the analysis of data in your study will be unique, if it does not involve standard statistics, if you have invented part of the procedure, you must describe in the proposal how it will be carried out. Perhaps you have a way of extrapolating trends that needs to be explained. You might have thought of a new method of depicting information that will allow easier interpretation. Tell these to the readers of your proposal.

Concluding Sections of the Proposal

The rest of the proposal pretty much depends upon the actual group to which it is addressed. In most cases you will want to summarize how you will go about reaching conclusions and to whom you intend to report findings. (Sometimes, by the way, you may not want to reach conclusions but merely to report findings and allow readers of your research report to decide for themselves what conclusions are justified.)

Prepare a time schedule in advance and make it realistic. (You can probably do this by doubling every time that seems reasonable to you, e.g. if collecting data should take two months, allow four months.) Set deadlines for yourself, but keep in mind that if this is a proposal for funded research you may be stuck with the deadlines you set.

Prepare the budget. Again, if this is a proposal for funded research you must do this very carefully because you will be stuck with it.

Put a bibliography and any appendix items needed on the end of the proposal and you are done.

SUMMARY OF REQUIREMENTS IN PLANNING YOUR RESEARCH AND WRITING A RESEARCH PROPOSAL

BASICS

Remember that all research, whatever type it may be called according to books on the subject, must include at least the following:
   1. Statement of a problem to be solved
2. Consideration of prior information related to the problem
3. Collection of data relevant to a solution for the problem
4. Analysis of the data and relation of findings to the original problem with a view toward stating a solution. These are minimum requirements, of course, and a specific piece of research usually has either additional refinements of one or more of these or additional items.

Problem Statement

Unless you are trying to solve an identified problem, you are not doing research; you are merely collecting information. But, identifying a problem nearly always begins with a kind of shotgun approach to the collecting of information, with the conducting of a literature search in a *problem area*. When you are ready to write a research proposal, you should have refined the problem area down to a single researchable question, however.

Typically, a beginning researcher (and some old hands as well) states too large a problem or one that is so broad that it cannot be solved in any reasonable length of time. (Example: Is scientific training valuable to the average student?) Discuss your research ideas with others in the same field, ponder what you would have to do to solve the problem you have in mind, think about the time that would be required to collect the information needed, and reduce the problem to one that can be handled.

State the problem as a question, and then, if possible, switch to hypotheses and think of the problem as a set of hypotheses that can be investigated.

Background Information

The key to refining a problem is finding those elements of an overall problem area which have already been solved to the satisfaction of most people and identifying those areas which are still unsolved. A further key to stating a good research problem is to find support for your own idea that a given problem is worth investigating. Finally, you should make use of whatever techniques or procedures have already been invented in attacking a research problem.

All of these are background information that you find by conducting a thorough search of the literature in your problem area. But, the *basic* is finding the information needed to refine the problem.

Collection of Data

With the problem statement as your guide, determine what information is needed to effect a solution. Think what would be required to answer the question. Think in hypothetical terms, and try to imagine what information would be needed to enable you to say that the research hypothesis is, indeed, correct (or, conversely, that it is totally wrong). How can you obtain such information? Do you need to devise an experiment in which you manipulate variables? Does the data exist so that all you have to do is find it? Will a description of some status quo satisfy the question, or do you need to locate a cause-effect relationship? Are you possibly concerned with being able to predict one variable from a knowledge of another?

This type of question will lead you to a specific design for your study, and the design, in turn, will almost dictate the data collection procedures.

However, you must also consider the validity of your study. What is the population? How large a sample is needed? What variables must be controlled? This type of question will help you to decide on the conditions of the study, the setting in which data is collected.

Analysis of Data

How will your data be handled once they have been collected? Will you table the information, categorize it, calculate certain statistics for it, or what? How will the data be related to a solution of the original problem? Will it directly solve the problem, or does it have some indirect bearing on the problem? Will you be able to state findings, or will you have to justify inferences? If the information turns out negative to what you had expected or hoped for, will you know something of value?

Who will benefit from knowing the results of your research? To whom should findings be reported? What generalizations can be made? What limitations prevent you from making broader generalizations? All of these need to be considered when you are planning your research.

In planning the study your basic consideration should be how a solution will be attained for the stated problem. You might foresee, for example, that your data could result in the identification of trends that can then be extrapolated into a solution. You might expect to be able to identify a cause for observed effects so that in future cases the effects can be predicted positively if the cause is present. Maybe your data will tell you that a theoretical explanation for a phenomenon is a good one, that it works.

REFINEMENTS

As suggested, each of the basic ingredients in a research plan may have refinements. As a matter of fact, it could be your ability to make such refinements that makes the difference between an acceptable plan and one that never gets approved.

Think of refinements in terms of the following:
1. Hypotheses
2. Techniques, instrumentation, validity, and reliability
3. Design variations
4. Statistics

Hypotheses

Not all research problems can be stated in hypothesis form. For example, many historical or descriptive studies are of such a nature that a hypothesis would be artificial. Also, the only hypothesis that might be possible in certain trend studies is, "There will be an identifiable trend . . ." But, if you can, you should state hypotheses in your proposal — underlying hypotheses if they are identifiable, research hypotheses certainly, null hypotheses if they are meaningful. The explanatory hypotheses may come at the end of the study after you have made some findings that need to be explained, or they may form the real basis for the research. (In many scientific studies the procedure will consist of stating an explanatory hypothesis for some phenomenon and then checking out the hypothesis by using it to predict some event and observing whether or not that event occurs.)

Techniques, Instrumentation, Validity, and Reliability

Your literature search may have included a portion of material that is useful in terms of planning how to conduct the research; this is good if it is needed. If any instrumentation is to be involved in the study, you need to describe the devices, give their validity and reliability, if available, and include copies as appendixes to the research proposal if possible.

In case you do not know for sure at the time of writing the proposal what data-collecting devices will be used, you at least need to tell how you will make this decision. If you plan to develop your own devices, you need to tell how this will be done and how validity and reliability will be established.

Design Variations

Selection of a basic research design from among those identified may actually be only the beginning in planning how you will conduct your research study. Most designs need to be modified in some way to fit the exact situation in which the researcher must work. Often in human research, random selection of subjects is not possible, and the design must be modified by some sort of cluster selection. An ex post facto study may not begin with identification of the "presumed cause" but may only have as the starting place the general question of what possible causes can be found in the historical data. Factorial designs can be set up in a great many patterns, so there really is no basic statement of this design. You might assume that a two-by-two setup is basic, and any deviation from this needs to be explained. Each independent (manipulated or assigned) variable should be identified, and its variations in the experiment explained. Obviously, the dependent variable needs to be identified, along with its measuring procedures. By the way, there can be more than one dependent variable also; each would constitute a new factorial design structure.

The ways in which your plan varies from standard should be explained in your proposal so that the reader will understand what is intended.

Statistics

As was pointed out, not all studies will have numerical information, but if your study does have such data, you should describe the statistical treatment you plan to apply to it. There is certainly no harm done by specifying in the proposal the formulas that will be used and/or the source of interpretive tables.

ADDITIONAL ITEMS

Anything in addition to the preceding that you can include in your proposal to make its intent clear will probably be worthwhile (subject to a limitation suggested in the upcoming personal note). Some people like to include lists of definitions for terms, particularly for technical terms not in common use. Some like to carry out a pilot study (a small scale tryout of what is proposed) and report its results in the major proposal. Some like to present a discussion of the significance of what is proposed in philosophical terms. Include whatever of these you like, and also include your own ideas for making clear the intent of your study.

I have been involved in numerous situations where I have helped to judge the worth of research proposals. A fairly common practice for funded research proposals is to have a panel of three or four readers examine the proposals and score them. Then, a second panel reads the proposals independently and scores them also. The final score is a combination of the two evaluations. Some things that have influenced me in reading proposals (and they have influenced others also) are as follows.

The proposal obviously has to fit the funding patterns of the agency. If you want to do something out of the line in which the agency is interested, you need to get advance agreement that your idea will be considered, or you will be marked low in the evaluation.

A long proposal turns the reader off. Sometimes the length is limited by the guidelines of the funding agency, and if you exceed this length, you are in trouble. In any case, it is very useful for there to be a concise abstract that tells in a nutshell what the proposal is all about. Be sure to write a *good* abstract like the ones I described earlier in this book.

Abstruse terminology and convoluted syntax are anathema to many proposal readers. (How about those terms? Did they turn you off right away?) Do not be afraid to use proper technical terms, but do not try to show your own intelligence by using complicated structures or by inventing and using your own unique language. Just describe what you want to do in straightforward sentences and paragraphs.

Perhaps the worst sin in a proposal is to fail to have done your homework. If the reader gets the idea that you have not really checked out your sources of information, that you have not consulted with known experts in the field, and that you are trying to get some money to *begin* your efforts, he will probably mark you down in the evaluation. (*I* would.) You should demonstrate in the proposal that you have a thorough grasp of the field in which you plan to study, that you "know what you are doing."

Another rather gross sin is being too elaborate. If a simple design will get the job done, that is what you should propose; do not try to invent involved procedures just for the sake of the procedures. Remember that the purpose of research is not in its doing but in its results; what counts is what you will have contributed to the store of knowledge in the world when you finish, not how you obtained that knowledge. (Well, I have to take part of that back. It does matter how you obtain knowledge, but you do not have to obtain it in a complicated manner for it to be worthwhile.)

Finally, be a bit humble. Give credit to others when it is due. Do not refer to yourself unless it is necessary for clarity. Emphasize the importance of the research rather than of the researcher.

SUMMARY: WRITING YOUR RESEARCH PROPOSAL

1. Cover page and title: If your proposal is for submission to a funding agency, use the cover specified. If the proposal is for a thesis or dissertation,

your college or university will, no doubt, have a style manual that you are expected to follow. It is probably best to leave the cover material until last, since it is minor in terms of content, and your ideas may change as you develop the rest of the proposal.

2. Basic problem area: If you have decided to include this in your proposal, rather than going directly to the specific research problem, it should be stated at the very beginning. Also, you should make it clear that this was the tentative problem area with which you began your study, not the proposed problem. Do be sure that the stated research problem grows out this problem area if you use it.

3. Literature search: This section should basically define the research problem. It may, however, contribute to the proposal in other ways. It may be used to suggest research techniques or instruments to be used in data collection or a design modification, etc. It is fairly important that this section provide a justification for the problem in addition to defining it.

4. Problem statement: The research problem may be stated at the end of the literature search or at the beginning of the next section, or both. It is probably best to ask a question rather than to say, "The purpose of this research will be . . ." The reason for this is twofold: first, a question rather nicely leads to a hypothesis, and second , a question is much more clear to the reader than a statement of purpose.

5. Hypotheses: If at all possible, state the research hypothesis and the null hypothesis. If you choose to explain the source of your research hypothesis, it might be good to state what has been called in this book the underlying hypothesis. If the nature of your problem is such that stating a hypothesis is impossible or awkward, be very careful to explain just what you are looking for as you proceed to collect data. What will guide you in the selection and analysis of data so that it will fit the problem?

In certain kinds of research, the hypothesis is absolutely essential. In this research what you are trying to do is determine whether or not a hypothetical explanation is a viable one; obviously, then, you have to describe the hypothetical explanation in detail.

6. Source of data: Your data will be collected from one of the following: (1) a chemical or physical system, (2) a structured observation of existing circumstances, (3) historical documents, (4) a sample of human beings, either directly for the sake of information on the sample or for the purpose of generalizing from the sample to a larger population, (5) a sample of other living organisms, usually for generalizing either to a larger population of the same organism or for generalizing to another organism group, (6) a sample of some system, living, nonliving, or a combination, or (7) some other data source. Whatever the source and the arrangements for sampling and sub-

sequent generalizing, you must explain very thoroughly in the proposal what kind of data you are going to collect, how you are going to obtain it, and what you will do with it after you have it.

    A. Describe the source itself.

    B. Describe the nature of the data to be collected.

    C. Identify any instruments to be used in data collection, tell their validity and reliability, incude a copy if this is possible.

    D. Describe any tabulating procedures or processes to be used in summarizing data prior to statistical analysis.

7. Treatment: If an independent variable is involved in your study in any way, its manipulation (treatment) must be described and related to the data collecting procedures of the preceding section.

    A. Controls: If any variables are to be controlled or if you are assuming that certain variables do not need to be controlled, this needs to be explained in the proposal.

8. Data analysis: Describe the way in which you intend to relate the data to a solution of the problem. What statistical tests will be utilized? What significance levels will be accepted? What will be the results of analysis; what will the findings look like?

9. Conclusions and "meaningfulness": You can describe the latter; to whom or for what purposes will the information learned in this study be important? How will the findings be reported? Discussion of the former, however, will be speculative. If this is found, then the conclusion will be . . .; if this, . . . then this . . . What are the limitations of the study?

10. Bibliography: A listing of all sources used in the literature search and in other parts of the proposal should be provided.

11. Budget and time lines: For those proposals which require it, provide a budget of expenses and schedule the events that need to occur for the research to get finished and the report to get prepared.

12. Appendices: Any material that is important to an understanding of the proposal but which has not been included as an integral part of the proposal should be placed in an appendix.

CHAPTER 5

CONDUCTING THE RESEARCH PROJECT

It might be good to think of your research project in terms of four phases for the main research and a fifth phase, which consists of a follow-up if you decide to continue the work. You need to (1) get organized, (2) collect data, (3) analyze data and draw inferences, (4) write the report, and (5) follow up. The first two of these will be discussed in this chapter. The others will follow in Chapters 6 and 7.

GETTING ORGANIZED

You might use the following as a sort of checklist in the organization phase of your project. Retype the list, modifying the sheet(s) with headings: date to be completed, date completed, not applicable.

1. Materials list (paper, supplies, chemicals, apparatus, organisms for culturing, media, etc.)

2. Materials purchased

3. Space arranged (lab space, office, work area for assistants and yourself, rooms for observation if needed, etc.)

4. Advance arrangements for computer time and help

5. Assistants identified and hired (or volunteers accepted)

6. Any staff appointments required made (In a university the process of hiring assistants and paying them, as well as the process of putting yourself on the proper budget, is rather complicated. You certainly need to check with the budget officer for help in handling these details.)

7. Any budgetary arrangements made, in addition to item 6

8. Data-collecting devices selected and purchased (Put these into two separate items if it is more convenient.)

9. Arrangements made for instructing assistants

10. Population described; if random sampling is to be used, population list assembled

11. Any needed approvals obtained (Some approvals may have been obtained in connection with preparing the proposal; check now to be sure that all needed permissions are arranged, such as the committee on research with live

animals, or maybe the SPCA, the committee on research with human subjects, the school system for educational research, individual principals and teachers, the subjects themselves after selection, parents if subjects are minors, owners of biological study areas, fish and game officers, if specimens are to be collected out of season or under protection, and whatever other permissions you might require. Each should be typed in the list separately so it can be checked off when arranged. Keep in mind that neither a parent nor a minor child himself can actually sign away his right to hold you responsible for injury due to carelessness or neglect, regardless of how you word the permission statement.)

12. Sample selected

13. Logistics for sample arranged (If the subjects are children, they need to be placed in proper classes or times for their observation and treatment need to be arranged, for example. If subjects are animals, arrangements need to be made for their housing and care during the experiment and for proper "disposal" afterward. For plants certain obvious arrangements are needed. For chemicals the chief concerns are with initial purchase of substances in the proper grade of purity, for storage and handling during the experiment, and for final disposal — particularly if there is any element of danger associated with them.

14. Schedule of treatments and observations established and communicated to anyone who needs to know (Again, you might prefer to put this into two separate items.)

15. Arrangements made for storage of data until time for analysis (One thing many researchers do, because they worry about losing very valuable information that may have taken a lot of effort to obtain, is to make copies of any printed or written information that is going to leave their possession. Audiotapes and videotapes can be accidentally erased; storage must be carefully arranged. Some data may be sensitive in another way, namely, that it should not be seen by anyone except the researcher; in research with human subjects, the right to privacy must be observed.)

16. Treatment materials prepared (printed materials, equipment to be used in treatment, chemicals, etc.)

17. Preliminary studies (A pilot study may be needed in order to validate and establish reliability of instruments; some preliminary data collection may be required in order to calibrate instruments and/or set handling techniques; a small scale "run-through" may be advisable to make sure that the whole procedure that has been designed is going to work; etc.)

As was suggested, it would be a good procedure to type a list like this one (including any items that may not have been listed here but which you need in your own plans) and use it as a checklist to be sure that all is ready for the treatment and data collection phase.

COLLECTING DATA

In Chapter 3 data collection was discussed in three categories: (1) automatic systems, (2) semiautomatic systems such as pencil-and-paper tests that have to be scored and interpreted, and (3) subjective procedures such as personal observation. The need for establishing validity and reliability of devices for collecting data was also discussed in that chapter. Consequently, what follows here is information and ideas related to specific techniques or instruments for collecting data. If you find that you need further information, for example, on how to do the statistical calculations needed to determine reliability of a test in a test-retest situation, you should consult a reference either on statistics, on research design, or on tests and measurement.

Taking Notes

It may seem unnecessary to say anything about taking notes, but a few pointers may be in order, nevertheless. For example, how many times have you sat in class and taken notes only to find two days later that you could not interpret what they said? Maybe you failed to record keys, perhaps your abbreviations were nonstandard, or was it just that your hurried handwriting was

Data Chart for Ecological Study

Date ————— ,   Recorder ——————— , Plot number ————

Species	Number in 100 m^2 Quadrat	Size Range	Comments
		Etc.	

Dominant species (from appearance) ————————————————

Largest species ————————————

Age of plot ——————— How determined? ——————————

————————————————————————————

Additional notes

indecipherable? Whatever was the problem, you want to be sure that any data recorded in the form of personal notes will, indeed, mean at a later time what you intended it to mean when you wrote it down.

It is strongly advisable never just to take notes. If it can be done at all, you should have a plan for note taking laid out in advance. In a biological experiment in which you make daily notes of observations, you could have a chart prepared with rows and columns specified so that in each box you would write a specific kind of information. On page 59 is a simplified version of such a chart. The idea of a chart could, of course, be adapted to fit many different situations in which you need to plan for note taking.

Notes should always be identified with at least two keys: (1) the date, time, and place and (2) the note taker. Your original notes should be stored after they have been translated and analyzed, until you are sure that you will no longer need to return to them for additional data or for clarification of something you have done. Stored notes can quickly become totally meaningless without identifying information.

If the notes to be taken are based on research reports, use the format suggested in Chapter 1 for abstracting. In this case it is not so vital that you identify the notes with dates; it is more important that you have the complete bibliographic reference so that you can return to the original source if you need to.

NOTETAKING IN HISTORICAL STUDIES

First, if the study is a trend study, you might be able to set up a data chart similar to the one suggested on page 59. You could prepare a categorical listing of the kinds of information you are seeking at least. Suppose that your study were related to the trends in provisions made by senior colleges in the United States for the special handling of students with handicaps — blind, deaf, crippled, etc. In looking for trends in such a case, your research problem would probably be something such as, ''What budgetary provisions must a college administrator make in this year's proposal for the handling of handicapped students in the coming biennium?'' You would then be looking for trends that suggest that certain changes may be required or advised, such as (1) structural alterations, (2) curriculum content, (3) course timing, (4) course scheduling, (5) instructor preparation, orientation, or reorientation, (6) hiring interpreters, and perhaps others. These expected problems, then, identify the categories of information you are seeking, and you can take notes *by category* as you read historical documents.

Ah, Ha! Didn't I tell you long ago that you should have hypotheses in your research plans? Now you see how it works in a case like this one. Having hypotheses allows you to look for *specific* information rather than for "just information." Your data collection is guided, aimed as a rifle is (or at least as a shotgun is) instead of just going off in all directions. Hypotheses are a *guide* to data collection. I must caution you, however, not to let hypotheses be your master. Especially in a study such as the one I was describing previously, a trend study, you must not let your original guesses (hypotheses) blind you to information that might suggest a totally new trend. What you need to do is modify your hypotheses as you go about collecting data so that the new hypotheses take into account new information that you have found. This will not change the usefulness of having hypotheses as guides to data collecting, and it will keep you flexible so that you won't miss some important information that doesn't fit into a category already established.

What I'm talking about is sometimes called serendipity, which means the finding of useful answers that were not sought. I suppose everyone knows the story of the discovery of penicillin, for example, in which a happy accident (leaving a Petri dish uncovered by mistake) resulted in the observation that a mold growth seemed to induce lysis in the staphylococci growing on the culture — something in the mold was killing the bacteria. Actually, the use of molds to cure infections had been known to the ancient Egyptians, and a doctor, Ernest Duchesne, had experimented with *Pencillium glaucum* and its effects on bacteria in 1897 (Fleming's discovery of penicillin came in 1927) but apparently serendipity was not operating. For inspiration, and perhaps to increase your own chances of making happy discoveries by accident, you ought to read one or both of a couple of books that recount stories such as that of Fleming.[1] If you get the book by Al Garrett, read the chapter on the discovery of freon to see both how *two* happy accidents contributed to this finding and how irreverent is the supposed high level theorizing of scientists at times.

Another approach in note taking in historical studies may be necessary if what you are seeking is not trends but rather historical description (the research question is of the type, "How far into northern Alabama did Spanish adventurers move in the early history of the American continent?"). A hypothesis is this case will not help very much in guiding research.

You can, however, use either the "continuous thread" or the "verification" process. In the first of these, you locate several historical documents that have promise of containing information related to your question, and you search them for any material that appears to lead in the direction of what you are seeking. For example, you might find that a Captain Solano was known to have stopped for provisions at an Indian village in northern Florida in a given year. This can serve as the beginning of a thread. You next look for other accounts of the travels of this Captain Solano in an attempt to see if he crossed over into Alabama and, if so, where he went. Having found, say, that he did

[1]D.S. Halacy, Jr., *Science and Serendipity: Great Discoveries by Accident* (Philadelphia, Mcrae Smith Co., 1967).
Alfred B. Garrett, *The Flash of Genius* (Princeton, D. Van Nostrand Co., Inc., 1963).

enter what is now known as Alabama, you might be led by your thread to information sources that tell more about that particular part of the state. Perhaps the captain ventured still farther, or perhaps some of his men remained and branched out to explore on their own.

The verification process might involve hunches (which are a kind of hypothesis). Suppose that in the same question as before you found a note in a military diary that Easter Sunday was celebrated on the southern shores of "Lake Charles." Suppose also that something in the context of the diary leads you to think that this is not a reference to Lake Charles in Louisiana, but rather to some lake whose name is now different. The verification process would lead you in two directions. First, you might search for confirming data that the lake referred to was not the present Lake Charles (a verification of your hunch). Second, you might try to discover the past nomenclature of a variety of lakes that seem to fit the description of "Lake Charles" in the diary. If Lake Charles eventually turns out to be a lake in central Alabama, you have moved in the direction of solving your problem. Then you have to locate still other sources of threads or ideas that can be verified until you are satisfied that you have exhausted the possibilities and found the farthest penetration of the explorers into Alabama.

Questionnaires and Interview Guides

Much data for surveys and other descriptive research will come from firsthand interviews (in person or by mail) with individuals. (Your description may not be of a sociological situation, of course; it may be of a physical system. In the latter case what follows regarding questionnaires and guides will still be applicable with appropriate modifications.) As before, your data collection — note taking — should always be guided by some advance idea of what you want to find. You should also not be bound by whatever guide you decide to use, but be alert for serendipitous opportunity.

CHECKLISTS

Perhaps the simplest device for data collecting in this type of study is the checklist. Just make a list of the things you expect to find or that need to be observed if the research question is to be answered. Provide either for checking them off or for enumerating them in the case of frequency being important. Following is an example of a checklist in part related to a survey of laboratory facilities for high school instruction in chemistry.

Quantity	Item
_____	Workspaces for students
_____	Sinks
_____	Balances, triple beam
_____	Balances, analytical
_____	Sets of standard reagents (HC1, H_2SO_4, HAc, NaOH, NH_4OH, HNO_3)
_____	Sets of beakers (400 ml, 250 ml, 100 ml, 50 ml)

QUESTIONNAIRES

There are several important points to be kept in mind if a mailed questionnaire is to be used. First, it must be easy to answer, or your returns will be very small. You can make a questionnaire easy to answer by at least three techniques: (1) make responses multiple choice, (2) use statements and an agree-disagree response scale (a Likert type of scale), (3) place statements on cards and use a sorting device of some kind, a Q-sort.

Everyone understands multiple choice. A Likert type of scale has respondents checking where they fall on a scale such as: Agree strongly, Agree, Neutral, Disagree, Disagree strongly. In a Q-sort respondents are asked to sort the cards into piles of specified numbers; for example, take forty cards. First select the ten whose statements you agree with most strongly. Then select the ten whose statements you disagree with most strongly. Place the remaining twenty cards into a third pile. Of the twenty ''neutral'' cards select three that you almost agree with and three that you almost disagree with, or three cards for which your feelings are not strong on each side. Now take the ten ''strong agreement'' cards and select five that you could be persuaded against or for which your feelings are least strong. Add these to the pile of three ''almost agree'' cards. Then take the pile of ten ''strong disagreement'' cards and select the five with which you could be persuaded to agree or for which your feelings are least strong. Add these to the three cards identified as ''almost disagree.'' You now have a set of five piles of cards — Agree strongly(5), Agree weakly(8), Neutral(14), Disagree weakly(8) Disagree strongly(5) — in a kind of normal distribution. You can attach scores or values to the cards and perform numerical analyses of various kinds to interpret the data.[2]

Second (with regard to questionnaires), it must be easy for the respondent to get the form back to you. If he has to provide his own envelope, address it, and stamp it, he is not very likely to go to that trouble and expense. You should provide return envelopes.

Third, unless something in your study demands identifiable data, you should guarantee anonymity of respondents. Do not place a ''name'' blank on the form, and avoid other identifying questions. If you need demographic data, this can be obtained without the individuals' identifying themselves by name.

Fourth, if you can ''pay'' respondents, you will get better returns. The simple way to ''pay'' is to offer to provide a summary of the results of the study when it is completed. Place a blank on the questionnaire for the respondent to complete (and, of course, you will need his name and address) if he wants this summary; not too many will choose to receive the report, but offering it will get you better responses.

---

[2]This is only a very rough example of Q-sort. If you decide to use the technique, consult other references such as the following: W. Stephenson, *The Study of Behavior* (Chicago, University of Chicago Press, 1953). This was the original. Or, Fred N. Kerlinger, *Foundations of Behavioral Research*, 2nd ed. (New York, Holt, Rinehart, and Winston, Inc., 1973).

INTERVIEW GUIDES

A questionnaire, of course, could serve as an interview guide. All that would be different is that the interviewer would ask the questions and mark the answers. If you follow the preceding procedures you will be conducting a *closed interview*. A guide for an *open interview* might consist of questions such as, ''What is your favorite color? Whom would you nominate for president if you had the choice? Which TV program do you watch most often?'' and the like. The choices of answers are open rather than limited. Naturally, the problems presented with this type of interview data appear in the analysis. Tabulations will be much more difficult when any answer is acceptable than it is when the answers are limited. The advantage of an open interview is that the respondent may come up with new points that you had not thought of — with serendipitous opportunities.

What is frequently done is to use a combination of open and closed responses in the interview. Ask a closed question: ''Do you prefer TV program A, B, C, D, or E?'' and follow it with an open question: ''Is there any other program that you really like better than any of these; if so, which one?'' Or, follow a choice question with the question, ''Why did you choose this one?'' This way you can easily tabulate the basic information and you still have the opportunity to discover interesting variations from what was expected.

RECORDING INTERVIEWS

You might think that a good simple technique to use in collecting interview data would be to make audiotape recordings of both the questions and the answers. The problem is, however, that (1) many people do not like to be tape recorded and (2) many will not be as truthful if you are recording their actual voices as they will be if you are just taking notes. Besides, you will have to interpret the recording eventually anyway, so you might as well write down the answers as they are given. Note taking is to be advised over recording, unless you will need the recording for later verification or for interviewer reliability checks.

In conducting some interviews with young children, a research group of which I was a part used specific guides (called protocols), which were handled almost like a script. We did not *read* the questions, but we tried to say exactly the same things in the same way each time. Also, each closed question was followed with an inquiry into the reasons for the choice. The following is part of the protocol guide for this research.[3]

TASK 3 (Conservation of Number)

   E shows S some red and black checkers, and says, ''Watch what I do. I'm going to make a row of black checkers.'' E then proceeds to make a row of eight black checkers.

[3]Charles C. Matthews and Darrell G. Phillips, *Handbook for the Application of the Science Curriculum Assessment System* (Tallahassee, Florida State University, Department of Science Education, 1968) p. 18.

E says, "I would like for you to make a row of red checkers beside the row of black checkers, but I want you to make your row so that there is one red checker for each black checker."

E then hands S all the red checkers. After S has completed his row of red checkers S will have some extra red checkers, and he may admit that there are too many red checkers on the table. E may take the extra red checkers from S only if S agrees that there are too many red checkers.

If S cannot make the equivalence between the two rows, or does not admit to there being extra checkers, then E should say something to the effect "Are there the same number of red and black checkers?" E should not force S into the establishment of equivalence, but should gently question as to the number of red and black checkers.

If S still does not admit to the equivalency of the two rows of checkers or cannot establish the equivalency of the two rows of checkers then the task should be terminated and E should go to the next task.

If the S does establish the equivalence of the two rows of checkers then E should remove all excess checkers (those not in the two rows) from the field of view. Then E can proceed with the questions: "Are there the same number of red and black checkers?" then, "Why do you think so?"

Then E says, "Watch what I do. I am going to move the black checkers." E then proceeds to move the black checkers into a group and asks, "Are there more red checkers, more black checkers, or are there the same number of red and black checkers?" Then, after response, "Why do you think so?"

Then E says again, "Watch what I do. I am going to move the black checkers once more." E then proceeds to arrange the black checkers into a long row parallel to the red row. This row of checkers should be 1½ to 2 times as long as the red row.

Then E asks, "Are there more red checkers, more black checkers, or the same number of red and black checkers?" Then, "Why do you think so?"

Regarding recording interviews, we did not tape-record the subjects during interviews used for data collection. We did, however, prepare a set of videotaped interviews to use as reliability checks for interviewers and to use in instructing new interviewers in proper techniques.

CONSTRUCTING QUESTIONNAIRES AND INTERVIEW GUIDES

The basic concern in developing guides is that they must obtain for you the information that you need to answer your research question. A secondary concern is that they do this job effectively and efficiently. The whole problem is one of content validity, and for this type of instrument, it is best solved by using the *jury technique*.

You write an original version of the instrument and present it to two juries, a group of experts who can say whether or not the instrument has content validity and a group of persons like those who will constitute the eventual sample in your research study. The information you want from the latter group is whether or not the instrument "makes sense," whether its terminology is clear and unambiguous, whether the responses fit the questions, whether it is too long, too short, too personal, whether there is any reason that it will be spurned (if a questionnaire) or not answered truthfully.

What you want from the former group is specific information regarding validity so that you can modify the instrument for a second trial. Find out from this jury the following things:

1. For each item in this instrument check whether it is valid, not valid, or neutral for obtaining information that bears on the research question.
2. For each item, can the jury members suggest a better way of wording it that would obtain more precise or more useful data?

3. Should the total instrument be (a) shortened, if so what should be cut out, (b) lengthened, if so what specific questions should be added, (c) restructured, if so what order is suggested?

You should also consult a reference on test construction for pointers on how to state items to avoid ambiguity, how to make them unbiased, what to do about technical terms, etc.

Observational Data

This section began with comments regarding the taking of notes. Now consider more specifically the recording of data from observations in sociological settings, i.e. with human subjects. You might consider five basic procedures: (1) narrative recording of observations in continuous fashion, (2) frequency recording, having a list of items to look for and recording the frequency with which each occurs, (3) time recording, having a list of items to look for and recording which is occurring at the end of each specific time interval, (4) sociometric recording, noting interactions among persons in the group, and (5) using a mechanical device to record the whole situation for later analysis. The last, of course, is a different type of recording category from the others. Presumably you could use procedure 5 and then analyze the information through use of procedures 2, 3, or 4.

NARRATIVE RECORDING

Narrative recording in a classroom, for example, can be done by taking "minutes" in meeting style, recording the important happenings. This requires a lot of judgment and introduces possible observer bias into the data. Perhaps a better technique is to record continuously what is going on without trying to make any judgment regarding the importance of events. This means that the observer either has to be able to write very fast or can utilize some system of shorthand to get everything down on paper.

FREQUENCY RECORDING

In this procedure a checklist is prepared in advance showing the specific behaviors to be recorded. If you were recording the data in a group meeting, as of an organization, for example, the categories might be as follows:

Opinion is expressed
Motion is made
Motion is seconded
Motion is discussed
Vote is taken
Objection is made to statement of chair
Objection is made to statement of member

Announcement is made

etc.

Then a tally is made by an item each time it occurs during the observation period.

TIME RECORDING

Perhaps the most famous system for recordng observer data is the Flanders Interaction Analysis System referred to earlier in this book. The original system was designed for observing classrooms and had seven categories of teacher talk, two categories of pupil talk, and a tenth category of silence or confusion. Many adaptations have been made of this system to fit unique observational situations.

You could, of course, devise your own observation instrument following the Flanders model. The key elements are a checklist of expected behaviors and some provision for the unexpected so that any resulting tallies made with the instrument will be interpretable in terms of percent of time devoted to a given behavior. The time interval for tallies made with the instrument should be short (as was mentioned earlier, the Flanders instrument involved three-second intervals) so that the data may be presumed to be unbiased.

SOCIOMETRIC RECORDING

When the study is concerned with attitudes of individuals toward one another, the type of data needed may be termed sociometric. A variety of means for collecting such information has been Pinvented (and you can invent still more procedures if you need to). In one procedure you simply ask the individuals to list in order of their preference the other members of the group. In another you ask, "With whom would you prefer to work as team members to solve this problem?" You might also add, "With whom would you least like to work?"

In still other techniques you produce a set of questions to which individuals are to respond with names of fellow group members, questions such as: "If you had a personal problem, with whom would you discuss it? If you needed help on ——— whom would you ask? Whom would you prefer as president of your group? etc." Or, you describe a person. (This person is kind and gentle, friendly toward strangers, and open minded. He is intelligent and will always do his best when given a problem to solve.) You ask group members to name the person you have described.

You can also record sociometric data from observations, using a checklist or other techniques already discussed. The data then are analyzed in terms of interrelationships among group members.

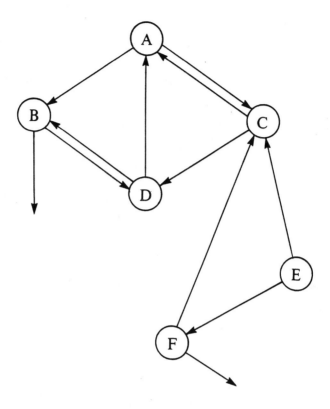

In a research study done some years ago, I used sociometric data collecting techniques. The setting was a high school chemistry class, and what I asked was for each student to list three other students that he would prefer to have assigned as his laboratory partner in the order of his choice. They were told that assignments would actually be made from these lists, but not everyone could be assigned his first choice, in all probability. After a period of "treatment" consisting of work especially designed for a new procedure utilizing the laboratory, students were asked to make the lists again, in terms of, "If you now had to choose your laboratory partner what three persons would you select in rank order?" By comparing data before and after treatment, I then had some idea of the effects of the treatment on this type of choice. For example, I was able to show that there was a significant correlation between demonstrated laboratory ability and likelihood of being chosen by a large number of peers in the second case, where this had not been true in the initial data. My personal comment: Sociometric data is easy to obtain and difficult to analyze.

TAPE-RECORDING DATA

In 1961 Oscar Lewis, a professor at the University of Illinois, published a book,[4] which was the result of a research study conducted almost entirely by means of audiotape-recorded data collection. Some tests were used in the study, but the bulk of the information presented was recorded on audiotape in the voices of the original ''cast of characters.''

The book is an analysis of the life-style of *los pobres* in a Mexico City slum — a real family (not named Sanchez). The ''new style'' used in the presentation is that the stories of the four main individuals in the family are told in their own words. Doctor Lewis indicated in the book that this was possible only through tape-recording, since the individuals were illiterate and certainly could not write their stories, but they could tell them orally.

Audiotape-recording and videotape-recording incidents or whole situations offer an opportunity for verification that is much more difficult with other methods of recording data. The exact information, rather than some interpretation of it, can be stored indefinitely and referred to again and again. Different individuals can analyze the information, and reliability can be established by correlating their results. In some cases it may even be possible to clarify data; a subject whose comments were recorded can listen to them himself and indicate the intent or meaning of what was said.

Recording has two disadvantages. The first is that the presence of the machinery for recording may bias the data, but this is also true of human observers — their presence, too, may cause subjects to behave differently than they would normally. You overcome this problem by blind recording for a period of time until the subjects ''get used to'' the observer or tape recorder and no longer act for it. The second disadvantage is that the data must *still* be interpreted by a human listener after it has been recorded, and the whole process requires at least twice as much time as a firsthand observation.

Videotape recording can be used in some rather unique ways in data collecting, and you often find unique things that might not otherwise have been discovered. In a continuing research project that began about 1968, we used videotape to record data. We had a class of young children who were being taught science content by special procedures. We set up three video cameras, one focused on the teacher from the students' vantage point, one focused on the class from behind the teacher, and the third focused on an individual student who changed every five minutes by random selection (we hung numbered discs around their necks and randomly selected the numbers to be taped). In analyzing the data we viewed all three tapes side by side and could thus get three different viewpoints of exactly the same situation; sometimes this was very enlightening.

In the same project we used videotaped instruction for part of the class on certain days each week. We then videotaped the students watching the TV (we set our camera behind the TV set so that, in effect, we were

⁴Oscar Lewis, *The Children of Sanchez* (New York, Random House, 1961). A prior research publication by Lewis was similar in procedures: Oscar Lewis, *Five Families* (New York, Basic Books, Inc., 1959).

looking back at them looking at us) and used the data thus collected to modify our presentations.

We also used videotapes for instruction of teachers in the project and for the training of data analysts and observers.

Test Data

Much of the data collected in educational, psychological, and sociological research comes from paper and pencil tests, or possibly from tests administered in other modes. A test must measure the variable that is intended to be measured, or it is of no use. It is important to note that a test that has been reported valid in one situation may or may not be valid in another; it is valid only if the variable being measured is the same in both situations. Otherwise, validity must be reestablished for the new case.

If your research requires data that is best collected by means of a test, you have two possibilities: you can locate a test to use, or you can devise your own test. Locating a test should be fairly simple, since a variety of published sources is available. Just ask your reference librarian; you will find books listing achievement tests,[5] attitude tests, aptitude tests, self-concept tests, intelligence tests, projective tests, and just about any other type of test you might need. Also, most libraries have files of the tests themselves that you can examine under controlled conditions.

In locating a test to use in your study, be sure that it meets all of the following criteria: (1) it must measure the variable that you intend to measure, (2) it must be valid for that variable, (3) it must be reliable, (4) it must be applicable to the group that you will use as subjects — age level, language, terminology, difficulty of items, etc., (5) it must be simple enough for you to administer and score it, or you must have access to someone who can do these for you, (6) it must be in published form so that you can purchase copies, or you must be able to obtain permission from its owner to make copies and use them.

Also, you should study possible instruments carefully so that you select the *best* one for your purposes, not just the first one available or the one most easily handled.

WRITING YOUR OWN TEST

If you are forced to develop your own test you really need to consult a reference on test writing, unless you have already had experience in test design.[6] In case you have had some experience at test design, a few pointers will be given here.

[5]An example is Oscar Buros, (Ed.), *The Eighth Mental Measurements Yearbook* (Highland Park, N.J., Gryphon Press, 1978).
[6]One resource is Norman E. Gronlund, *Measurement and Evaluation in Teaching,* 3rd ed. (New York, The Macmillan Co., 1976).

First, it is assumed that what you need is a norm-referenced test, one in which any individual is compared with the total group that takes the test. (The other alternative is criterion-referenced tests, where the individual is compared only with himself, with his earlier performance or with what is expected of him in terms of mastery.) If this is the case, it is strongly urged that you develop a test that can be objectively scored; ordinarily this suggests a multiple choice test rather than an essay examination. Essay examinations can be made objective, but the process is involved and will probably require several helpers to assist you in scoring, since the basic procedure is interscorer reliability estimation. (By the way, true-false and matching test items can be included in multiple choice tests very easily; they simply have only two choices in the former and as many choices as there are potential matches in the second case.)

Suggestions regarding multiple choice tests follow:

1. Determine the nature of what you want to measure with the test. Presumably this is content information, but there are many kinds of such information. Check Bloom's *Taxonomy of Educational Objectives*[7] for precise information on categories that need to be considered.

2. A test is a sample of the content that it presumes to measure; it can hardly ask every conceivable question but only a very limited number of them. Thus, you need to be sure that your test (a) has items representing each major category of information that it is supposed to measure and (b) does not contain extraneous items, items that are not a legitimate part of the expected information.

3. Each test item itself should meet the following criteria: (a) the item is of a difficulty level appropriate to the test takers' age level, intelligence level, reading ability level, etc., (b) the stem and possible responses are so worded that the test taker is not prevented from responding correctly, is not misled — if he knows the answer, he should not be led to think that he is wrong, (c) the item does not contain obvious clues to the answer so that a person who does not know what

is being asked can still get the item correct (a "Who is buried in Grant's tomb?" type of question), (d) there should be only one correct answer; distractors should be plausible but, nevertheless, unambiguously wrong.

You need to establish validity of your test; the jury technique for doing this has been described earlier. You also need to establish reliability and you have probably already built a pilot study into your research plans for this purpose. (Again, check a reference on testing for procedures used for establishing reliability.)

A doctoral student of mine conducted a dissertation study in which part of the work consisted of developing a new test. What he wanted to meas-

[7]Benjamin S. Bloom (Ed.), *Taxonomy of Educational Objectives, Handbook I: Cognitive Domain* (New York, David McKay Co., Inc., 1956). There are also two other taxonomies in the series: *Affective Domain* and *Psychomotor Domain*.

ure was the cognitive ability, evaluation, so that he could compare students who took a traditional chemistry course with those who took one of the modern courses (CBA or CHEM Study) on this criterion. No test to measure this trait existed, so the student had to invent one, validate it, and establish reliability before he could carry out the original study. If it seems that it might be of help to you, you could examine his dissertation.[8]

SOME CONSIDERATIONS REGARDING THE USE OF TEST DATA

Assuming that you have a valid and reliable test that does indeed measure the variable that you intend to study, the quality of your data will depend upon the situation in which the test is given and upon the scoring and interpretation of results. A test is an "obtrusive" measure for human characteristics, just as an x-ray may be an obtrusive measure for atomic-sized particles. The measuring device may contribute to change in the things it measures. Having taken a given test, you will probably perform differently on the same test if you ever take it again — you will have learned some bit of information from the test, you will have undergone an attitude change of some sort, or you will have attained a set toward the test or its contents. Thus, any test-retest situation automatically has the potential for biased results. Furthermore, you nearly always need to give a test twice to a group of subjects; either you need to repeat the test for establishing reliability, or you need pretreatment data so that you will be able to attribute cause to the treatment, or you must repeat the testing to measure retention of material learned.

Random selection of both the experimental and the control group from the population will enable you to avoid the necessity for pretesting, but with human subjects, random selection is usually not possible. Making sure, then, that both experimental and control subjects are treated in exactly the same way in the testing process is important. It would be wise to establish a protocol (such as one discussed earlier in this chapter) to be followed when the test is administered. This way you can be sure that everyone gets the same instructions for the test. You also need to be sure that the attitude with which subjects approach the test is the same for both groups. If one group thinks that a part of their grade depends upon performance on the test and the other group does not have this belief, they are likely to perform differently because of this factor alone. Both groups must be given the same reason for taking the test (even if you have to tell a white lie).

If one group knows that it is part of an experiment, particularly if it knows that it is the experimental group, and the other group does not know this, the performances may be affected. (This is the so-called Hawthorne effect.) Again, test protocols, strictly adhered to, should help solve the problem. By making

[8]John Schaff, "Assessment of the Cognitive Ability *Evaluation* in Students of Conventional and Modern High School Chemistry." Unpublished doctoral dissertation, Florida State University, 1968.

sure that the groups are alike, you have not, of course, removed the problem of obtrusiveness. All you have accomplished is to be more sure that any final differences between groups are not due to obtrusiveness itself.

The major obtrusiveness problem remaining is the one related to generalization. When you attempt to apply to the larger population whatever you have found in the sample, you must keep in mind that the population will not have been pretested. Thus, whatever the effect of obtrusiveness, it needs to be "subtracted" from the generalization. There is not any good way to do this, although there are ways to find out whether obtrusiveness is a significant factor or not. The Solomon Three Group and Four Group designs for educational research are ways of handling this problem; so is the factorial design in general, since it can detect interaction effects and determine their significance. If you find a significant obtrusiveness effect, you must be very careful in generalizing to a population; if the effect is not significant, all you really need to do is keep in mind the same "uncertainty" regarding your generalization that the scientist thinks of in his measurements.

SCORING TESTS

The objectivity of a test is really in its scoring rather than in its construction. Objectivity means the degree to which the score obtained is independent of the scorer, and this is why it was pointed out earlier that an essay test can be objective if the proper procedures are carried out.

Perhaps the best way of ensuring objectivity is to have a test that can be machine scored. Your *key* will still be subjective, depending upon your judgment of the correct answers, but at least every test paper will receive the same treatment if it is scored by machine. Second best is to use a punched key so that your scoring is still essentially automatic, and third best might be to have a secretary or assistant score the tests (someone who has no particular interest in the outcome).

Unobtrusive Measures

A polygraph may be considered essentially an unobtrusive measure of "truthfulness." It does nothing to the person being interviewed (except perhaps to make him a bit more nervous). Actually, according to a recent article,[9] the polygraph measures the subject's belief in the truthfulness of what he says, not the objective truth of his statements.

A thermometer is an obtrusive measure of temperature; it absorbs heat and in doing so, changes that which it is measuring. Observing color and comparing it with a standard would be an unobtrusive measure of the temperature

[9]"Lie Detector is Increasingly Used as a Tool." The *New York Times*, April 8, 1980.

of a piece of hot metal. An unobtrusive meaure, then, actually measures something other than the actual characteristic of interest; it measures a consequence or concomitant of that characteristic.

As a part of our recreation, my wife and I teach couples to "round dance." In the teaching, the couples dance in a circle, and we demonstrate in the center the new dance or the new steps, or whatever. We can tell how insecure the dancers are with a new set of instructions by the size of the circle. When they are insecure, they close in on us and dance close together; when they are more secure, the circle is larger and the couples are farther apart. The size of the circle is an unobtrusive measure of security, in this case. I must admit that I have never done research with such an unobtrusive measure, however.

If you find, identify, or invent an unobtrusive measure to use in your study, you will avoid the "uncertainty" problem. You will, however, have the problem of establishing validity. You will have to convince people that what *you say* measures the variable does indeed measure it.

CHAPTER 6

ANALYZING AND INTERPRETING DATA

To many, the analysis of data means the statistical handling of numerical information. This is, of course, a correct thought, but it is certainly not inclusive of all that "data analysis" means. This chapter does not pretend to be a treatise on statistical analysis; for this kind of help you will need to consult a statistics book, a statistician, or possibly a computer specialist. Rather, the intent in this chapter is to present some general ideas on the handling of data and some specific suggestions to guide you in your selection of procedures for interpretation.

PURPOSES OF ANALYSIS

What are you trying to accomplish by your analysis of data? First, you are trying to answer the original research question. If you stated hypotheses, you are trying to describe evidence in support of the research hypothesis or in refutation of the null hypothesis (ordinarily). You may be trying to describe a situation or event or a series of events. You may be trying to identify trends. You may be looking for evidence that variations in one characteristic can be used to predict variations in another characteristic. You may be looking for evidence that a given variable is the cause of changes in another variable. Or, you may simply be looking for evidence that you can say, "Yes, it happened as I predicted it would; therefore, my theory is viable."

Sometimes the last of these is very simple. You may have stated a theory, described an expected event based on the theory, set up a situation that would be expected to result in observation of the event, and looked to see if it happened or not. The data may consist simply of evidence that the event occurred — pictures, recorded information, eyewitness accounts, etc. The analysis of such data requires little except restating it in terms of the original problem. It may not be nearly so straightforward however, and you may have to subject the data to extreme analysis just to demonstrate that the expected event did occur.

Whenever analysis is more complicated than simply restating information, it may be helpful to think in terms of the following things you can do to data. You might recognize in this list the general principle of *simplification*.

1. Reduce data to fewer units of information.
2. Relate information in one unit to that in another unit.
3. Compare data from one or more units with a "standard" (commonly the

standard will be the research hypothesis or the null hypothesis).
4. Combine data from several units to describe
   a. events
   b. situations
   c. sequences
   d. trends
   e. predictor-predicted variables
   f. cause-effect relationships

The last of these, while it does involve *simplification,* is also a creative step and includes *synthesis* as part of the process of relating the data to the original problem. Thus, the whole procedure of data handling is analysis (simplification of information) followed by synthesis (recombination into a new format).

REDUCING DATA

A simple first step in reducing numerical data is combining like information, tabulating into frequency tables. The big step, however, is the calculation of single descriptors for large amounts of information. The mean and standard deviation (or variance) are descriptors for a whole set of test scores, for example. (There are other descriptors, depending upon the type of numerical data with which you must work.)

How do you reduce verbal data? First, it is extremely important that you do reduce verbal data; it is simply not possible to interpret a string of words and sentences, except a very short string. Begin by asking yourself, "Why did I collect this piece of information?" Having asked yourself this several times, you will see that there exists (probably existed from the beginning of your data collection) a set of categories into which you can now classify your information.

If your research is historical, you may have collected information *by event,* this is, you may have several sets of data all related to one event and other sets related to another event, etc. So, to begin your reduction of data, you could classify the data by event. Another unit of organization for historical data is time; you might place all information for a given time period together. Still another unit might be source; you might benefit from this kind of categorization when sources are likely to be biased in their presentation. For example, an account of the practice of slavery (even though a primary source, say a diary[1]) written by a Southerner may be different from a similar account written by a Northerner.

In status quo descriptive studies you are likely to have information related to specific situations or locations or organizations, etc. It is the same with trend-seeking studies, longitudinal studies, and others. Think of your

[1]A diary may be a primary source if it records eyewitness accounts or a secondary source if it records impressions gained from other than eyewitness. In either case, however, it may be biased; even the eyewitness story can be colored by the feelings of the observer.

categories; you may even want to list them before beginning to analyze the data.

As in handling numerical data, where the *mean of means* and the *standard deviation of the difference between means* have specific and important meaning, it is important to consider combining categories in a second step of analysis. Alternatively, it may be advantageous to recategorize, to look at the information in a different format, when handling nonnumerical data.

You can also *count* pieces of information in nonnumerical data. Three of your sources said this, four said that, five said still another thing. This is something similar to considering a vote. Some researchers count the number of times a given term is used for a specified meaning and the numer of times for a different meaning in trying to interpret their information.

A variation of counting might be called "weighing." You can consider the amount of verbiage devoted by a source to a given topic in comparison with other topics and interpret this to mean a greater or lesser amount of importance attached to the topic. You can also consider a large number of sources reporting a given event in comparison to smaller numbers reporting other events as a measure of the importance of the events in question.

In summary, for nonnumerical data, *categorize*, *count*, and *weigh* information in order to reduce it to more usable form.

RELATING DATA

Relating data from two sources literally means placing the two sets of information side by side and seeing how they look in comparison with each other. Mathematically, you can subtract (this one is this much smaller than that one) or divide (this one is so many times as large as that one) for comparison, as long as you have pieces of information that can legitimately be manipulated in this way. You can compare means and standard deviations (or variances), you can compare standard scores but not raw scores (except from the same test). You can draw graphs and compare them (as long as the axes are identical). And so on.

But how can you relate nonnumerical information? First, you may be able to use arithmetic as in the preceding example. If you counted or weighed information, you would have numbers that you can relate. Do not, however, try to make interval data out of what is really nominal data (unless you build a strong case for doing so). This means that it will be OK to say that one item is lesser than another in importance or value but not to say that one is five times as strong or as important as the other.

You can also draw graphs. This would be important in trend studies where you are looking for *growth* in some characteristic, *repetition*, *decline*, *disappearance-reappearance*, etc. The graph would be a pictograph if the data is not numerical, but it can be used nevertheless.

If you have absolutely no numerical basis for comparing (or relating) two pieces of data, the very least you can do is to "lay them side by side" figuratively and read them and then say, for example, "This information leads to that (in a logical sense)." Or, "This information follows that (in a chronological sense)." Or, "This seems to depend upon that (in a cause-effect sense)." Or, "These are simultaneous." Other statements can also describe what you have found, including the statement that there is no relationship.

COMPARING DATA WITH A STANDARD

The standard of importance is the hypothesis, although you may find use for certain other standards such as the "norms" for a standardized examination. You can think of comparing your data with a hypothesis in each of the following ways.

1. The hypothesis is a prediction (based on theory) that a given event will occur; the comparison is to note that the predicted event did or did not occur.

2. The hypothesis is a statement that a predictor-predicted relationship will be found between two (or more) variables in the sample examined; the comparison is to determine a relationship (usually, but not necessarily) in the form of a correlation coefficient or a regression equation and then to decide whether or not this relationship meets a criterion for significance.

3. The hypothesis is a null hypothesis that there is no relationship of a predictor-predicted kind between the variables in question in the population that the sample examined represents; the comparison consists of determining the probability that, if the null hypothesis is true, whatever relationship was found in the sample could have occurred by chance, by random selection of the sample from the population.

4. The hypothesis is a statement that a cause-effect relationship will be found to exist between two (or more) variables in the sample examined; the comparison is to demonstrate the degree of applicability of the following: (a) when the presumed cause is present the effect always occurs; (b) when the presumed cause is not present the effect never occurs.

5. The hypothesis is a null hypothesis that there is no cause-effect relationship between the two (or more) variables in question in the population that the sample examined represents; the comparison consists of determining the probability that, if the null hypothesis is true, whatever cause-effect relationship was found in the sample could have occurred by chance, by random selection from the population.

6. The hypothesis is that the sample examined is (research hypothesis) or is

not (null hypothesis) different from a described population; the comparison consists of determining the significance of observed differences between the population and the sample, of determining the probability that observed differences could have occurred by chance.

7. The hypothesis is a more complex one than any of these, perhaps involving interactions among variables which, in turn, have some effect upon a dependent variable, so that under varying conditions varying cause-effect relationships are found; the comparison consists of an analysis of variance or covariance with follow-up analyses to determine the significance of any observed differences among members of the sample with respect to the measured (dependent) variable.

8. Other hypotheses than those named previously can be stated (although most will fit one of these categories); the comparison will have to be designed to fit the actual nature of the hypothesis.

Each of the types of hypothesis named can be compared with either numerical data or verbal data; in nearly all cases the numerical comparison will yield far more viable conclusions than the verbal comparison. (You are much more likely to be believed if you have numerical data.) In the following sections, each of these comparisons is discussed in more detail, with the emphasis on numerical comparisons. (Again, for needed statistics consult appropriate other references or experts.)

Theory-prediction Comparisons

The theory-prediction was actually alluded to earlier in this chapter. An example of this type of comparison might be the following.

The watchers in an unusual laboratory located in what had been the racquets court underneath the spectator stands of Stagg Field at the University of Chicago on December 2, 1942 were not really prepared for a celebration. They had to sip their wine from paper cups. What were they celebrating?

It was the culmination of the Manhattan Project in the successful self-sustaining controlled release of nuclear energy (sometimes called a chain reaction) that had been predicted by Enrico Fermi. The story began in 1939 when Otto Hahn and Fritz Strassmann accidentally (serendipity again) discovered that a sample of uranium that had been bombarded with neutrons contained barium, an element much lighter than uranium. Eventually, Lisa Meitner and Otto Frisch (also German scientists like Hahn and Strassmann, but working in Sweden because they had fled Nazi Germany) explained this finding by suggesting that the uranium nucleus splits upon bombardment into lighter elements. The process was named fission, splitting.

Following the explanation, it became obvious that the process of fission, since it produces additional neutrons, could be set up in such a way as to be continuous. Once the process was started, the neutrons from the first split could cause a second split, and so on. There were lots of complications, as you might guess. The process was not self-sustaining in nature because natural uranium contains only about 0.7 percent of the fissionable isotope U-235 and the common isotope, U-238, absorbs neutrons, thus preventing them from reaching another atom of U-235, even though atoms of the fissionable material might be available. Also, the whole thing was an *explanation*, a theory invented because observations had been made that did not fit any existing theory.

So, after inventing procedures for isolating large amounts of U-235 and after postulating the idea of "critical mass" (a certain critical amount of U-235 must be present in close proximity for the neutrons produced in one reaction to reach other atoms and cause them to split), the Chicago group of scientists had set up the apparatus that they *said* ought to allow for a sustained chain reaction releasing nuclear energy. Here, then, was research based on theory — with a vengeance. The theory was a powerful one; an awful lot of effort and money had been expended to develop the materials and apparatus to test it, and the "test" was simply to bring together the critical amount of U-235 and see if indeed a sustained release of energy resulted.

This all sounds very simple, but the structure of the original "pile" was quite complex. For example, the uranium was placed in packets throughout a mass of graphite, some 400 tons of it, so that the surrounding material could be used to moderate the speed of some of the neutrons. Also, the pile was permeated with cadmium rods, which also absorb neutrons and so could be used to stop, slow down, or speed up whatever reaction was occurring due to neutron movement. Anyway, it worked! That is why the wine was there — to celebrate the success — but they forgot glasses, and that is why paper cups were used in this world-shaking celebration.[2]

In the ideal theory-prediction comparison you will find that the predicted event either did or did not occur. In most real cases, however, you will probably be faced with something less straightforward, and your job will be to *convince* your audience that the event did occur as predicted.

Now I am going to express a personal bias. There are those who argue that the kind of research represented by the comparison just discussed is the only activity worthy of being called research. If they do not actually make this argument, they try to pattern their own research and to guide the research of others in this way. The feeling is that all research must be based on some theoretical foundation, that a research question is worthwhile only if it contributes in some way to greater understanding or applicability of the underlying theory (or if it brings about a change in the theory), and that research actually consists of doing what I have been dis-

[2]Adapted from Paul G. Hewitt, *Conceptual Physics: A New Introduction to Your Environment* (San Francisco , Little, Brown and Co., 1971) pp. 510-515.

cussing in the previous section making predictions on the basis of theory and then setting up situations in which you can determine whether or not the predictions "come true."

What this does is insist that all research must fit the mold of scientific research. What it results in is what are sometimes ludicrous attempts to consruct theories for systems that can have no theoretical base. In the physical world there are phenomena that can be explained by the invention of models (ideas) underlying behaviors. When you move to biology, theories are still useful in most instances to explain events. But, a theory must assume *regularity,* or it can hardly be used. (How could any model of behavior of atoms predict events if sometimes atoms behaved one way and other times they behaved differently and the differences were capricious?) As soon as you get into the "mental behavior" part of biology, particularly if the behavior in question of that of humans, it is hard to make up models that will take into account all of the variables the organism utilizes.

Why are there so many different theories in psychology instead of just one or two basic ones? Psychology is not too far removed from the physical sciences. Think of the situation in anthropology, or history, or art. How can you ever imagine that a theory or a limited number of theories could be invented to explain the behaviors of groups of people in all cases?

I do not mean to argue that no one should invent theories in these areas; many have and many of the theories have been useful. The theory of cultural lag, for example, is useful to explain many situations in the education versus the technology of a culture, and some economic theories have been very useful in making predictions of the consequences that would follow a given action. However, I just do not believe that there will ever be one or two theories that explain all of anthropology, for example, or all of sociology, or all of education. Also, I see nothing wrong when a field of study develops on the basis of paradigms for action rather than on the basis of theoretical explanations. Furthermore, I see nothing wrong when a field of study develops essentially by the accumulation of information. "Urban studies," for example, as a modern field of study may consist of nothing but an accumulation of information related to the life and structures in cities. I am not sure that it *needs* to consist of anything else.

My argument, then, is that there is not any validity to the contention that research must be based on theory; research done for the sake of accumulation of information is perfectly valid and likely to be as useful (indeed, often more useful) as research based on theory. Do not let anyone tell you that if your research is not theory-based, if its analysis does not consist of what I have discussed about predicting an event and then observing to see whether it occurs, it is not good research. Also do not let anyone push you into inventing theories if that is not your natural inclination. You do not need a theory to do research.

Predictor-predicted relationships

In any kind of trend study or correlation or prediction study, your basic hypothesis is that there is some variable that can be used to predict changes in another variable. You may believe that there were historical events that indicate a trend in the thinking of individuals over some time period and that, if you can discern this trend, you can be on the alert for a reoccurrence and make a prediction of some future event. You may have reason to suspect that two variables frequently occur together and that if you can measure changes in one of them you will be able to predict changes in the other.

Your hypothesis may be stated in research terms: there will be a relationship . . . . In this case it is related to the actual sample that you are measuring. However, the hypothesis may be stated in null terms: there is in the population no relationship . . . In this case you are set up for inferring that whatever you find true of the sample will also be true of the population it represents. If you calculate a correlation coefficient or a regression equation to depict the relationship, you will use essentially the same technique for comparison with the hypothesis, whether the hypothesis is positive or null. You will examine the significance of the statistic.

In the case of a correlation coefficient, you will simply look into a table and find significance. With a sample of 100 cases, for example, you would find that any value for the correlation coefficient above .23 is significant at the .01 level. If you had found a correlation coefficient of, perhaps .45 (well above the value specified), you could interpret this to mean either (1) that the relationship between the two variables measured is not likely to have occured by chance alone in the sample used or that there is likely to be a real relationship of some sort between them all at the .01 level of confidence, or (2) that, if there is indeed no relationship between the two variables in the population from which your sample was drawn (or more correctly, which your sample represents), the probability that you could have randomly selected just the right individuals to show the correlation that you found is 1 out of 100. Both of these results came out of the same table; the only difference is in how you approached it, what hypothesis you stated at the beginning.

Another way of thinking of predictor-predicted variable relationships is in terms of common variance in one accounted for by variance in the other. (''Accounted for'' is a term used in this connection, not in a *cause-effect* sense, but only in an observed sense; observed variance in one variable predicts a certain amount of variance in the other.) The percent of common variance is equal to the square of the correlation coefficient. For the .45 correlation coefficient mentioned before, the percent of common variance would be 20 percent. In a prediction research study, what you want to find is not only significant relationships but also large amounts of ''accounted for'' variance. You see, even though the .45 correlation mentioned before may be significant at the .01 level, it will be dangerous to use the variables to predict one another because so much of the variance is not common between them.

What you want to find, for a two-variable situation, is a high value of the correlation coefficient and a low value of the probability (significance). If you find one variable that "accounts for" some percentage of the variance in another, you can then search for a second that will account for still more of the variance, and a third and a fourth as necessary. (In this case you also have to be concerned with the common variances among the predictor variables. See the following figure.)

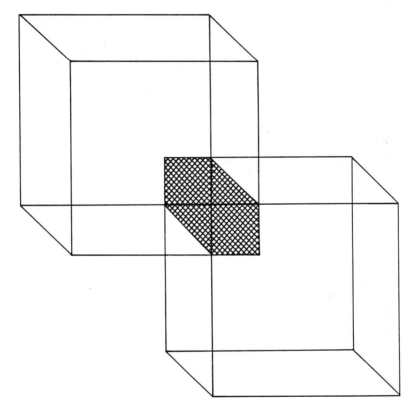

How do you do all of this when you do not have numerical data, mostly in trend studies or other descriptive studies? You go back to what was discussed earlier — categorize, count, and weigh your information. Lay the information on the two variables side by side (figuratively or in your mind) and see where they have commonalities. You can even estimate a kind of percentage of overlap between them in some cases; treat this estimate as you would the variance accounted for mentioned previously. Of course, all arguments in this case have to be verbal, you cannot look in a table and find significance, but you can still describe how one variable predicts another.

Do not forget the possibility of graphing. Plotting the occurrences of a variable will tell you something, particularly when you are looking for concomitant trends, which is the basis for trend study conclusions.

Cause-effect Relationships

Whether or not you can infer cause-effect relationships from a set of information is as closely tied to the design of the study that got you the information as it is to the manner in which you perform the analysis. You *do* need evidence that (1) when the cause is present the effect occurs and (2) when the cause is absent the effect does not occur. Ordinarily the way you set this up is to manipulate only one variable at a time, holding constant other pertinent variables, and then try to demonstrate that this manipulated variable produces changes (which you measure) in the effect variable. It is this kind of relatively simple design that is discussed in this section. (This type of study, by the way, does not have to be divorced from the theory-prediction type discussed in this part of this guide; the idea for the cause-effect examination can certainly come from a theoretical base — it can also come from mere speculation or from a literature search or other sources.)

If the experiment has been properly set up so that it has internal validity,[3] the analysis of data is fairly straightforward.

The information you are looking for is, ''Is the experimental group different from the control group on the variable identified as the *effect*?'' You made the groups different on the *cause* variable, and you controlled the other pertinent variables, so if you can demonstrate that the two groups are now different on the effect variable, you can say that there is, indeed, a cause-effect relationship between them.

Numerous tests can be applied to determine the differences sought. The binomial test, the sign test, the chi square test, the F test, the t test all measure, or rather determine, probabilities associated with observed differences. This is what you must find. You can never tell by looking at two scores or two means or two variances whether they are *really* different or whether the observed difference could have occurred by chance. Herein lies the problem with interpretation of verbal data when you are looking for cause and effect relationships. You have to observe close ties, or gross differences between outcomes, in order to be able to convince others that you have found a cause and effect situation. For example, two test means (same test) of 45 for one group and 46 for another, are they ''really'' different? No? What if they were 44 and 47? Still not? Would 43 and 48 satisfy you? Or 42 and 49, or 41 and 50? Where does it stop? That is what your analysis should tell you.

[3]See D.T. Campbell and J.C. Stanley, *Experimental and Quasi-Experimental Designs for Research* (Chicago, Rand McNally & Co., 1963) pp. 5 and 6.

What it will actually tell you is the probability that, if there is indeed no cause-effect relationship between the variables, the observed difference could have been found anyway — by chance. If you are dealing with a population hypothesis, a null hypothesis, the statistic will tell you the probability that, if the null hypothesis is true (if there is no cause-effect relationship between the variables in the population) you do still have two groups that represent that population even though they display apparent differences on the effect variable; the observed effects occur by chance some percent of the time without the ''cause.'' Earlier in this book the setting of significance levels was discussed. Whatever level you have decided is appropriate for your research is the level you are seeking now in order to be able to say, ''I have found significance at the ———— level,'' or ''I reject the null hypothesis at the ———— level.''

How do you decide which test of significance to use? In this business of rejecting null hypotheses, notice that you have the possibility of making either of two types of errors. Type I (so called in all statistics books) is rejecting a null hypothesis when you should not have done so, when it is actually true. Type II (also a common term) is failing to reject a null hypothesis when you should have done so, when it is actually false. You do not *want* to make either type of error, but you cannot help yourself. The probability of making a Type I error is the same as the significance level, so you can reduce the likelihood of this error by setting a very low significance level. The problem is that when you do this you increase the likelihood of making a Type II error.

The probability of making a Type II error is related to the size of the sample, and it decreases as the size of the sample increases. The power of a statistical test is defined as the probability of rejecting the null hypothesis when it ought to be rejected, when it is actually false, which is exactly what you want to do. Power is equal to 1 minus the probability of making a Type II error. Power is related to the type of test chosen, so you should examine the power of possible tests and choose the best one for the size sample that you have used.

Choice of a test also depends on the kind of information that you have available. If your data is ratio or interval, for example, t tests and F tests are appropriate, but if the data is ordinal, these cannot be used. You need to look at the assumptions of the test proposed and decide whether your data meets these assumptions or not.

Finally, of course, you should choose a test that you understand. You will have to interpret whatever you find, and if the test is mysterious to you, you will find interpretation difficult — and defense impossible.

CAUSE AND EFFECT IN STUDIES WITH NONNUMERICAL DATA

As was pointed out earlier, it is difficult to establish a ''real'' difference between two groups if there is no numerical information on them that you can compare. You have only two choices: either base your difference arguments on verbal information or obtain numerical data in some way. If the first of these is what you must do, try to base your arguments on *large* differences between the two groups, on semihard data such as individual case studies, rather than merely on group descriptions, or on the cause-leads-to-effect but cause-absent-never-leads-to-effect situation. (If this can be demonstrated, you are in good shape; if it can only be approached, you will have to argue.)

One possibility for getting numerical data out of purely verbal information is the model technique. You describe a purely hypothetical model and compare each of your real groups with it. Hopefully, you will be able to describe the real groups in terms of "greater than" or "less than" the model with respect to some number of characteristics. Treat each "greater than" as a plus and each "less than" as a minus and you have numbers. You can count the pluses and minuses, and use some appropriate statistic to compare the groups (perhaps a chi square). Then, if the experiment had been set up so that a difference between the groups could only be accounted for by reasoning that the treatment *caused* such a difference, you will have demonstrated the cause-effect relationship.

Comparing a Sample with a Population

If you know the characteristics of a population and you have data on a sample from that population, you can compare the two sets of information to determine whether or not the sample truly represents that population. This is basically what the t test is designed to do. In practice, the t test is more often used to compare data from *two* samples with each other so that a statement can be made that the two samples do or do not represent the same (hypothetical) population. (The z value can also be used for this comparison.)

Sometimes these techniques are useful in the preliminary stages of a research study as described; a variation of the situation occurs, however, as a frequent question in the analysis of data at the end of a study. Most often it is a chi square situation. Suppose that in the studies related to the eventual recommendation that saccharin should be taken off the market as a potential cause of cancer in humans something like the following had been done.

Fifty mice were fed heavy doses of saccharin daily for two weeks while a control group of fifty mice from the same genetic line were fed nonsaccharin foods. Over their lifetimes the mice were observed to suffer from cancer: ten of the saccharin group and three from the other group. The question that has to be answered is, "Are the ten out of fifty cases in one group significantly larger than the three out of fifty cases in the other group?" One way of approaching the answer is to assume that the smaller number of cases is "normal" and to compare the larger number with it to determine the probability of its occurring by chance. This is a chi square problem in which the population would be described as having a cancer expectancy of three out of fifty, and the sample of mice with cancer experience of ten out of fifty would be compared to it.

In this case the population was hypothetical (although the basis for it was simple reasoning) rather than known. Sometimes the population might actually be known, and the same technique could be used with even greater confidence. Suppose, for example, that you had collected the opinions of a large sample of people in the United States regarding some political candidate, and suppose that you wanted to find out if the opinions of men were different from those of women in the United States. Knowing the ratio of men to women in the total population (census figures), you could use this ratio and compare with it the ratio of men to women regarding opinion on any item in the opinion poll.

What has been described is the "goodness of fit" chi square; chi square analysis is also useful for "independence" of information. In this case, you do not compare a sample with a known or hypothesized population, but rather, you compare one dimension of the sample with another dimension. See a statistics reference for details on this technique.

Interactions

Analyses of variance and of covariance allow for the discovery of interaction effects among more than one independent variable. They also allow for the discovery of "main" effects, that is, the overall effect of the independent variables and of each of them separately. You can find the effects of independent variables separately in a multivariable experiment by calculating a number of t tests, but you cannot discover interactions in this way.

Thus, if the result you are seeking has to do with any sort of interaction among "causes" you need to use analysis of variance. (A word on interaction: this simply means that whatever the effect of a given independent variable on the dependent variable is, this effect may be modified by the presence or absence or the level of a second variable. The interaction can involve more than two variables.)

When to Retain the Null Hypothesis

In some instances in research situations, it may be desirable to find evidence that the null hypothesis is true. A good example is in comparing two groups prior to treatment. In this case you want the groups to be identical on certain pertinent characteristics, and if you use a statistical test to examine their likeness (rather than using matching, which presents problems in terms of the numbers of subjects required), what you want to do is to retain the null hypothesis.

Sometimes in the outcome of an experiment it may be desirable to retain the null hypothesis.

I once carried out a study in which I compared the performance of a group of chemistry students who had been taught using a new course with the performance of a norm group of students who had been taught using the "traditional" course. The comparison was made on scores on the College Entrance Examination in Chemistry, and you can see that this was a vital question. Would the students in the new course be penalized (or might they do better) in comparison with traditional course students when it came to applying for admission to colleges? If it should turn out that the students were likely to be penalized, something would have to be done about it — either in changing the examination or in changing the course back to the traditional one.

I would have been happy to find that the null hypothesis could not be rejected in this case, for this would have let me say that the students in the two groups did equally well, and I could then have justified the use of the new course on grounds other than test achievement. Of course, I would have been even happier to have found that the new-course students did better on the test than the traditional-course students. What I actually found, unfortunately, was that the new-course students *were* penalized, they did more poorly on the examination than their traditional counterparts.

The point is that this was a case where I really wanted to retain the null hypothesis.

In cases like this, the conservative researcher will make it difficult for himself to retain the null hypothesis, just as in the usual case, he makes it difficult for himself to reject the null hypothesis. This means that in setting a rejection level he will choose a high probability, perhaps in the range of .10 to .25. Doing this makes the probability of making a type I error high; the probability of rejecting the null hypothesis when it is actually true will be from .10 to .25.

COMBINING DATA (SYNTHESIS OR INTERPRETATION)

The final step in conducting research is to synthesize the information gathered and analyzed and use it to answer the original question. (Of course, you still have left the writing of the research report — the subject of the next chapter.) You should be very careful here to separate what you have *found* from what you are willing to *infer*; information cannot be refuted, although someone else might find counterinformation, but inferences can be made independently by anyone who has the information on which to base them. What you should do is answer the original question to your own satisfaction but leave it open for anyone else to answer, using your data, in his own way.

If your study is descriptive of a status quo, you should put together the information obtained and describe whatever it was that you set out to describe.

Describe "the average chemistry laboratory used in high schools in the United States," for example. But, if you want to infer from this description, for example, that improvement is needed in some specific way in the high school chemistry laboratories of the country, be careful. Unless your original question was, "Are high school chemistry laboratories . . . adequate to do . . .?" you are going beyond the research study in making the "needed improvement" inference.

In a historical study, you should gather together all of the information and present the historical account that you sought. As mentioned before, if you want to make inferences from this account, remember that they are your inferences and that someone else reading the same account might not accept them. The same is true for trend seeking and longitudinal studies of a descriptive kind.

Remember the famous case of the research that led to the newspaper headlines proclaiming "DEWEY DEFEATS TRUMAN," an incorrect inference.

In any kind of predictive study, your desired outcome must be to produce some sort of formula (be it mathematical, graphical, or verbal) that will let you and others make the prediction you sought. Going beyond this and making certain predictions, however, is exceeding the bounds of the study (unless, of course, your original question asked for specific predictions). So, with cause-effect studies, when you have demonstrated the relationship you have "done your duty." What is to be done about it is making an inference, and while you may want to make this inference for yourself, it may not at all be appropriate for you to impose it upon others.

In the study I mentioned before where I found that the students who had taken a new chemistry course did less well on a college entrance examination than traditional students, I inferred that the examination ought to be changed in order that it might be fair to all and that, in an interim period while it was being revised, there should be an adjustment factor added to the scores of the new-course students. Others with the same information, however, inferred that the new course should be scrapped.

I must admit that I was not as careful then as I am now suggesting you should be in separating inferences from information. I was not pleased with the counterinferences, since I was interested in promoting the new course, and I still do not think that they were right, but they *were* valid.

Finally, in a theory-based prediction study, you have done your duty when you can say, "Yes, the prediction did come true; *I* therefore infer that the underlying theory is viable, and I will continue to use it." If you go further and suggest, for eample, some of the ways in which the theory can now be used, you are going beyond your research and getting into what is called follow-up in the next section.

I must close this section with the admission that not everyone agrees with me in these last few points. There are those researchers who say that you *have not* done your duty until you have told others what your findings mean, which involves making inferences. What you had better do is not take either my advice or theirs but find out what is the belief of those to whom you are going to present your research findings — your major professor, your colleagues, your journal editor, your funding agency; then you may find that you have to compromise between their beliefs and your own.

FOLLOW-UP

In the last section you were warned against going beyond your original research problem in making interpretations of data collected. This is what you probably ought to do. Most research, while it contributes to the store of knowledge in the field, also leads to the realization that there is more that needs to be learned. It is to be hoped, therefore, that you have come to this realization with respect to your study and that you want to continue your research. There are several basic ways to do this.

One thing you can do immediately is to reconsider some or all of your data to see if it answers questions other than the one you set out to answer. Recategorizing your information in new ways might suggest the questions, or reading over what you have found may suggest questions to which the data speaks. The beauty of this kind of extension of your research is that it does not require going through the whole proposal process again, although it probably will involve an additional search of the literature (for the same reasons that you did the original search).

Many researchers prepare articles reporting on *parts* of their research project so that they can present several publications out of one effort. The reason for this is not necessarily the cynical one of getting more mileage out of the work; not too many publications will accept long articles, such as the one that would result from a major research study. It is necessary to break the study down into pieces to get it published.

Another extension of your research might result from considering the limitations you had to place on your original study. What would occur differently if . . .? (if I had a larger sample? if I could randomly choose subjects? if the treatment were applied for a longer time? if the subjects were a different age? if a different organism were used? if the soil conditions were changed?and so forth.) This type of extension would, of course, entail a whole new research proposal and all that goes with it, except that you already have a head start.

As was implied in the preceding section, some of the inferences you want to make from your data may well apply beyond the research question. This situation suggests the need for additional research. Make the inference; this then becomes the theoretical base for a new prediction of some event, and the prediction needs to be "checked out."

Still another extension possibility is in serendipity. In the February 18 issue of *Chemical and Engineering News,* an interesting story was recounted telling how two researchers had accidentally run across a situation that led to a totally new piece of research.[4] The two doctoral students involved were collecting caterpillars to add to the university collection when they found a unique larva with long tentacles on its tail. They took it home to observe further and in the course of events noticed that it seemed to respond to certain musical sounds by flicking the long tentacles up over its back. To follow up on this observation, they went to a laboratory and made systematic observations to determine just what sounds had this effect.

In a second accidental discovery, the researchers found that some of the caterpillars had been parasitized by wasps (not an uncommon event), and they had an expert identify the specific wasp involved with the long-tentacled caterpillar. Considering this wasp, they found that the wing beats produce a sound at the pitch which had been found to excite the caterpillar. This led to the hypothesis that the waving of the tentacles might be a defense mechanism.

In following up this lead, the researchers found that the tentacles contained flagellae with storage sites similar to those in another caterpillar in which such sites were known to store formic acid. The theory then developed that the caterpillar waves the tentacles to surround itself with a cloud of formic acid to repel the wasp.

Moral: Always be prepared as you do research for the serendipitous event, for something out of the ordinary that just might lead to new discoveries. By all means take the time to follow up on your hunches, on your new questions, and on offbeat ideas.

[4]K. M. Reese, Newscripts column. *Chemical and Engineering News,* 58:120, Feb. 18, 1980. (Washington, D.C., The American Chemical Society).

CHAPTER 7

WRITING THE RESEARCH REPORT

The final stage of your research project consists of publishing your results, reporting your findings to other people. Ordinarily this means the preparation of a *formal* paper of some kind, and it is this formal report that is the subject of the first part of this chapter. Any of seven types of report might be the one you have to write: (1) thesis or dissertation, (2) report to a funding agency, (3) report for "consumers," (4) report for other researchers, (5) article, (6) monograph, (7) book. Specific suggestions for each of these will be given later in this chapter.

GENERAL POINTS TO BE CONSIDERED

In writing the report, whatever the type, you should always keep your audience in mind, just as you did with the proposal. Indeed, it may be the same audience. Your writing should be pitched at the level of the expected readers, using the terminology appropriate to them and using syntax that will be understood readily. The research report is not, regardless of your pride of achievement, the place to "show off" your superior knowledge by speaking down to your readers or by using abstruse language and convoluted structures. If you do this, they simply will not read the report (and they will mark you as a snob at the same time). Perhaps you can retain your humility by keeping in mind all of the things you now realize that you *do not know*.

Should you use the technical language of your research field, or should you try to simplify it and write in more commonly used terms? The answer depends entirely upon the intended audience. If you write for chemists, they expect you to use the chemical terms with which they work every day. If you write for sociologists, you should use sociological terminology, but if you are trying to relate to a group of sociologists what you have found in a piece of chemical research, you had better minimize both kinds of terminology. You probably are not very familiar with the one and are likely to make blunders, and your audience will probably not understand the other. So, just write in "plain English" as much as possible.

Should you define terms when it is *necessary* to use technical language? Again, the answer depends upon the intended audience. You certainly should not define a term for someone who already understands it, and you *should* define it for those who are not likely to be familiar with it. You should always define abbreviations that you feel you must use, even though they may be common knowledge among your readers (except very common abbreviations such as ml, g, lb., tsp.). This is because your report will go beyond your intended audience, and you will not want it to be totally mysterious in any aspect to the new reader.

If you define a term, you should do so the first time it is used (either in the text or in a footnote), or it should be included in a clearly identified glossary or list of definitions. If possible, the definition should be functional or operational rather than theoretical. Once again, you may need to provide theoretical definitions if your audience needs this type of understanding and does not already have it.

In terms of structure, it is better to err on the simplistic side than on the esoteric side of the continuum. Use two medium sentences rather than one long complex one. Keep the paragraphs short and definitely coherent so that the paragraph content is distinctly related. Use subheadings as necessary to clarify the structure. They break up the material into more readable units, and they give the reader a place to "dive in" if he does not want to read all of the material.

Be sure that you are absolutely accurate in all information presented. This is meant to be a respected piece of new information for the field of the study, and if it contains any misinformation, all of it will be suspect. If in doubt about any of your own ideas that you intend to state, have them checked by an outside expert. Or, if they are strictly ideas, in the sense of speculations, specify that this is the case and take responsibility for them as yours alone. If you quote someone else, be certain that you do so accurately. Use the exact words, and do not neglect to consider the context. Everyone knows that a quotation out of context can sometimes mean the opposite of what was intended.

Worry about your grammar, punctuation, and spelling. In some types of reports there will be an editor to make corrections in these areas for you, but you really ought not to rely on someone else, except maybe your spouse, your secretary, or a colleague, for grammatical correctness in your paper. Have a dictionary, a thesaurus or cross-reference book of some kind, and a book on English usage handy where you can refer to them as needed while you write.

Make sure that what you write tells the story you intend. Never ramble off into allied comments; stick with whatever point is being made at the time. Repeat points judiciously; do not make repetition mechanical or too frequent, but restating important points will serve to emphasize them. Remember what was said earlier about "weighing" as a way of interpreting verbal data. Summarize materials at strategic points in the narrative, at least at the ends of chapters and probably more frequently. List, tabulate, graph, do whatever is necessary to make more clear the message you want to communicate. Again, keep in mind your audience. Some may not be able to interpret graphs, for example.

GENERAL WRITING PROCEDURES

Make an outline. You have been told from grade school on that the way to begin a paper is with an outline, and you may or may not have followed the practice. In this case, however, it is a good idea to outline your whole paper before you begin writing it. This means a *point* outline not just a topical structure. Do this as follows:

1. Decide on the major topics you must manage, such as the literature search, the procedures description, the data presentation, the analysis, and findings and write these down.
2. Make note of anything else that you would like to include but are not yet sure of.
3. Look at, or imagine, the amount of material that you have to use in writing each section. Think in terms of subsections under each major category. Write these down.
4. For each section and subsection thus identified, write down the points that you intend to make. Use whatever format makes sense to you; write sentences, make lists, whatever.
5. Make additional groupings, which will turn out to be sub-subsections, by putting like points or related points together.
6. Now you have a point outline. Read through all of it, and see if it tells *you* the story you intended. Rearrange sections, add sections, change point statements, add new statements of points to be made, etc. until it does tell you the story intended.

This takes a lot of time, but remember that you almost have the paper written when you have completed this final point outline. All you have to do is "flesh it out."

As you are doing the outlining, do not neglect your original proposal. After all, you did tell in that proposal what you intended to do and you have now done it, so maybe the *basis* for your report outline should be your original proposal.

Writing "Drafts"

If you have done a good job with the point outline, you may be able to get by with only two drafts of the final report. Write the first draft (it is suggested that you type it yourself if you can and compose as you type) straight through. It may require several days of work, and you may have to do other jobs in the meantime, but avoid major breaks if at all possible. Do not write a chapter and then stop for a week before you write the next one. Writing in a short time span is perhaps the best way to ensure continuity of the writing and cohesiveness of the "story." If you write it piecemeal, it may end up looking as if this is exactly what was done.

Read through the draft, and write or type in any needed corrections and additions. Leave until later the rewording of statements if they are technically correct in this draft. Add the refinements in draft form also — bibliography, table of contents, appendices, introduction or preface, and a title page (perhaps others such as acknowledgments, list of tables, etc.) but do not do an index yet. Bind the draft in some way, even if only by a large staple at the corner, and make a copy. This can be expensive, but if the only copy you have (the original) gets lost in the next step of the process you will have to repeat it.

Present the draft to an outside reader for review and, if possible, editing. In some cases this step will be automatic; for example, in writing a thesis, your major professor and committee members will want to read the draft before the final version is prepared. If the step is not automatic, include it anyway; an outsider reading the material is far more likely than you are to discover glaring errors or omissions.

While the first draft is being reviewed, use your copy of this draft to write an abstract. Use the format given at the beginning of this book and write the abstract *from the paper,* not from your memory of the project or of what you have written. If you can write an abstract *from the paper* in the format given and if that abstract tells you and others to whom you present it for checking what you intended to communicate in the research report, you have done a good job. If this is not the case, you will have valuable clues as to where changes are needed in the report.

Abstracting your own paper, from the paper itself, may seem to be only busy work, but it is perhaps the best way to check whether or not the paper contains what is needed to make clear its intended message. It may not be *fun* to do this abstract, but it will certainly be worthwhile.

Now get the paper ready for the second (and hopefully final) draft, to be done by a professional typist, unless you are that good yourself. Use your copy of the first draft; type needed corrections and changes on separate sheets of paper, marking on the draft itself only minimally. Use the draft copy and the newly typed sheets of corrections to prepare a "cut and paste" version of the manuscript.

Read the cut and paste version carefully and write in any corrections still needed. Make marginal notes to the typist of how to space special items or other needed instructions. Give the draft to the typist with a full set of instructions as to spacing, margins, manner of footnoting, etc. (Of course, you have to make your own arrangements with the typist, but it is worth suggesting that there be an understanding that if the typist errs in not following any of these instructions the corrections will be made at the typist's expense.)

When you get the final draft from the typist, proofread it again (it is even wise to double proofread) and have all corrections made right away. Then send off the manuscript, or present it for approval, or whatever is required, but do this only after making another copy. Many copies may be required at this stage, but you should always make at least one, for the same reason as was given earlier.

SPECIFIC WRITING PROCEDURES

This section deals with each of the seven types of report listed earlier in this chapter. Each of them has peculiarities in its preparation or presentation of which you need to be aware. Obviously, a complete set of guidelines for each type of report cannot be given here, only some of the major points to be considered. Consult specific publications for each of the types of reports as needed.

Thesis or Dissertation

Commonly the term thesis is used for the major paper required as the result of research at the master's degree level and the term dissertation is used for the research report at the doctoral level. The first may be used occasionally to cover both levels. Both are very formal, highly specified reports. If this is what you are writing, you really *must* obtain a copy of the guidelines provided by your institution. If those guidelines and anything said here disagree, follow the institution's guidelines religiously.

In addition, there are published manuals that are commonly referred to in the university guidelines, and you ought to have access to one of these.[1] Surely then you cannot go wrong, with your university guidelines, a style manual, and this book in addition.

Ordinarily there will be published deadlines that must be met for approval of a thesis or dissertation. Pay careful attention to these, and allow yourself several days leeway; it invariably takes longer than you think it will to get a research report written in final form. Also, there will be specific approval forms required for signatures of your supervising professor and committee, deans, etc.

[1]W. G. Campbell, and S. V. Ballou, *Form and Style: Theses, Reports, Term Papers*, 5th ed. (Dallas, Houghton Mifflin Co., 1978).
Kate L. Turabian, *A Manual for Writers of Term Papers, Theses and Dissertations*, 4th ed. revised (Chicago, University of Chicago Press, 1973).
Others are also available.

The type of paper to be used may be specified. This is commonly bond paper of 16 pound weight or heavier.; placement of material on the pages (margin allowances) and the kinds of type that are acceptable may also be spelled out. Ordinarily someone will have been designated (sometimes called a ''bibliographer'') who will check your paper for adherence to this kind of requirement and who must also approve the manner of making copies. It is strongly recommended that you learn who this person is well in advance of preparation of the final draft, make an appointment to discuss your plans, and make sure that you understand all that you have to do.

In first draft form you will need copies of your report for each member of your supervising committee. When you deliver these, it will be highly advantageous if you can suggest when you will return to pick up the marked copy. Make the interval less than a week if possible. This places a deadline on the reading of the draft so that it will not just lie around unnecessarily, but it also allows a reasonable length of time for the professor to get the reading done.

When you get marked first draft copies back from your committee members, try to integrate all the suggestions into the next draft if it is at all possible. Keep the original marked copies; sometimes a professor objects to something that you said, forgetting that he told you to say it. Do keep in mind, however, that this is *your* research report; if you have stong opinions on how or what is to be said, stick to them. Defense is the name of the game in thesis writing.

Prior to all of this, you should have checked with your major professor numerous times to be sure that the manner in which you are proceeding is acceptable. He may want to see early drafts of such things as your point outline. He will certinly want to discuss with you your interpretations of data. What you want is to have your major professor on *your* side at the defense so that you have help in responding to the committee if necessary. Besides, he is responsible for supervising your research, and he will *want* to see you often to keep check on progress.

The style of typing and placement of headings, the use of capitals, punctuation, page numbering, all these details will be specified in your university guidelines or in the style manual used. It is essential that your final draft typist be familiar with all of these. Your university will probably have a list of approved (or at least of experienced) typists; you will be smart to select one of these. The typist may also be able to prepare the needed multiple copies. For most dissertations at least three official copies are required (two for theses) and these include the ''original'' and two *approved* copies. Offset-printed copies may be required; photocopying may be acceptable, other methods of making copies may be approved. You need to be certain that your typist knows how to make the acceptable copies. Actually you will want several more copies of the final version of the report than the number required, since your committee members should be given copies, and you will need several for your own use.

Thesis or dissertation manuscripts are expected to be perfect. Errors must be corrected in such fashion that they are undetectable. Drawings or illustrations not done with the typewriter are expected to be done in India ink. The use of tables and their numbering and how you handle appendices will also be specified in either your university guidelines or the style manual.

APPROVALS FOR THESES AND DISSERTATIONS

Theses and dissertations will require at least two kinds of approvals; the content of the report will be approved by your major professor and supervisory committee, and the paper itself, its physical makeup, will be approved by someone in the university hierarchy, usually the office of the Vice President for Academic Affairs or the Graduate Dean. Much of the preceding refers to getting the format approved; you do have to worry about this because you will be required to make changes until it is approvable. More important, though, is the approval of the content.

You should have worked very closely with your major professor in putting the thesis together, but remember that you also have to satisfy a committee that (1) the research was worth doing and (2) you understand what has been accomplished and the total process of doing the research. It is suggested that you write the thesis with the thought in mind that you will have to defend it. Be very careful of making statements that are not firmly supported with data, either from the literature or from your own collection of information. Be very careful of making inferences that are not strongly supported by analysis of data. As a matter of fact, it is wise in the thesis to put in "disclaimers" whenever there is some doubt about the strength of a statement. Say, "It appears to be likely from the data that . . ." rather than, "The data shows that . . ."

CONTENT OUTLINE FOR THESES AND DISSERTATIONS

Naturally your outline will depend upon the exact nature of the study, but a general thesis outline is as follows (they really follow the same format in most cases).

ACKNOWLEDGMENTS
TABLE OF CONTENTS
LIST OF TABLES
LIST OF ILLUSTRATIONS
Chapter I. INTRODUCTION
   Purpose of the Study
   Demonstrated Need for the Study
   Summary of Methods and Procedures

Chapter II. LITERATURE SEARCH
    General Background
    Narrowing the Problem Area
    Statement of the Research Problem
Chapter III. METHODS AND PROCEDURES
    Design of the Study
    Population and Sample
    Methods of Data Collection
    Data
Chapter IV. ANALYSIS OF DATA
    Description of Analysis Procedures
    Presentation of Results of Analysis
    Findings
Chapter V. DISCUSSION AND CONCLUSIONS
    Relation of Findings to Research Problem
    Limitations
    Conclusions
    Suggestions for Further Study
APPENDIX
BIBLIOGRAPHY
VITA

Report to Agency

A research report related to funded studies usually involves two reports, the description of the work and findings itself and an accounting of the fiscal affairs of the project. With very rare exceptions, th fiscal report format will be rigidly specified by the agency. Depending upon your locale for the project (in a university, in an industry, in private locale, etc.), you may or may not have responsibility for the actual preparation of the fiscal report. If you do have this responsibility, handle it as you do your IRS Forms (follow all instructions precisely).

The research report for an agency may also be required to follow a specified format; this is not usually the case, however. What you need to do in this type of report is to present a case to the agency (1) that you used their money efficiently and effectively, (2) that what you found was worthwhile, either in itself or in that it has potential for leading to even greater findings, and (3) that, therefore, you should be seriously considered for further funding in future research proposals. As a matter of fact, there are exactly the things the agency will be looking for in your report. Typically, they do want to continue funding those researchers who are efficient and productive.

With these points in mind, you can see that the report needs to contain elaborate descriptions of the procedures that will show how the money was used, not including dollar figures but showing the people involved and the nature of the work they did. You will also want to discuss equipment purchased with grant funds and its use in the project. This type of report will have a much heavier emphasis on procedures than many of the others.

Your sponsoring agency is, of course, interested in learning the results of your study. Here is where you must be very careful to learn the nature of your audience. Many times those in an agency who read the research reports do not have technical knowledge in the field of the research (though they do have technical knowledge of *research*), but many times the reports are sent out to be reviewed by persons who do have such technical knowledge. Unless you know how your report is going to be handled, you had better tread a fine line between technical language that may not be understood and talking down to a reader through simplifying your descriptions. As has been said earlier, worry about this as you write the report.

It will nearly always be to your advantage, whether it is asked for or not, to include with the report two abstracts, a technical one that could be used by the agency for informing the profession of your findings and an "everyday language" one that could be used by the agency for informing the general public of your work (a newspaper release type of abstract). Many times the agency will prepare such abstracts anyway, and it is better for you, who knows the study best, to prepare them. Use the format that has been suggested in this book for the abstracts, their difference will be in the language used.

SUGGESTED OUTLINE FOR AGENCY REPORT

Identification of Project. Your project was probably assigned a number; use this in all reports. Identify yourself (principal investigator) and the agency to which the report is directed. Give dates of grant award and termination. Use the title under which the research was funded. Give your professional affiliation, if any. Acknowledge the assistance of anyone who helped in preparation of the report.

Statement of Project Purpose. This is the "problem statement" of most reports. You do want to state the research problem in the usual terms, but be careful at the same time to describe the purpose in a broader sense. Describe the context of the study as well as the research problem itself.

Background. This is the "literature search" section, but in this report it should be minimized. If the agency is interested in whether or not you did a thorough background search, the interest was at the proposal stage. You no longer have to justify the problem; all you have to do now is provide whatever background will serve either (1) to clarify the results of your work or (2) provide actual information that was used in the research.

Methods and Procedures. As was said earlier, this should be a large section with detailed descriptions of what was done, how measurements were made, how data was recorded, etc. You *may* want to include the following section here if it would make more sense to the reader.

Data and Data Analysis. In straightforward format, present the data found and indicate how it was analyzed. The analysis, too, should be described in straightforward terms; assume that the reader knows the procedures so that all you really need to do is identify them for him.

Results. Findings should be presented in as complete and clear a form as possible. Do not make the assumptions of the preceding part of the report, describe everything in detail. Do not make "outside" inferences, however; stick to the actual findings in relation to the original problem. Your goal is to tell whether you did or did not solve the problem and, if you did solve it, what the solution is. Any further explanation of what these findings mean comes in the following section.

Discussion and Conclusions. Here is where *you* talk (instead of letting the data talk). Tell what the findings mean in terms of practical applications or foundations for further research. State the conclusions you are willing to draw from the findings; include any cautions or limitations of which others should be aware. Unlike a thesis or dissertation, this report should be strongly positive in making claims that the findings can be applied in specific ways.

Credits. If used, bibliographic references should be listed here. You should also give credit to persons, agencies, or institutions that contributed to the success of the project.

PRESENTATION OF THE REPORT

An agency report, unless the agency specifies otherwise, should always be bound, not stapled, and should have a cover that is heavier than the paper of the report, printed with full identification of the project inside the report. The binding should not be elaborate or look too expensive; this would suggest a waste of agency money.

In most instances a report of this kind should be printed in multiple copies. The agency will want several copies, you will want to supply copies to your colleagues, and you will eventually get requests for copies as the information regarding your findings is disseminated.

Report for Consumers

Whether or not you actually prepare this and the succeeding reports will ordinarily be your choice; the thesis/dissertation and/or agency report would have been required. If you decide to write for consumers, the first consideration is, Who are your consumers? Do you recognize the pattern? You always ask first, ''For whom am I writing this report?'' If they are your colleagues in a professional field, you will prepare one type of report, if they are the ''general public,'' it needs to be different. If they are professionals but in a different field than the one in which the research was done, the report may be still different. Because of this, it will be difficult to specify here how you should write such a report; the best that can be provided is a few suggestions.

1. The report should be nontechnical in terminology and description of procedures. Do *not* assume that the reader will know what you mean by a spectrophotometer or by multiple regression analysis. Do not use scientific names for organisms, etc.

2. The report should not give elaborate descriptions of either background or methodology. The reader will not care how you decided to do the study, only what you found.

3. The report should not give actual data or discuss how the data was analyzed. The exception to this is in reports to colleagues or other professionals whose interest may be in the actual data more than in the conclusions you want to draw from it.

4. The problem and the reasons for its importance should be emphasized. If you want your consumers to use your findings, you first have to show them a reason for wanting to know the findings.

5. The major emphasis should be on the answer to the research question. Tell what is now known that was not known before you did the research.

6. Also, tell your consumers how they might want to apply the answers provided. You can suggest inferences and/or applications in broad fields or in the specific field of the consumer audience.

7. If it is of interest, you can suggest how the research leads to still further research, but do this only in order to emphasize the importance of these particular findings.

8. Bibliographies and the technical aspects of more formal reports will only kill your readers' interest in your report. Avoid including anything that would demand a bibliographic reference.

PRESENTING CONSUMER REPORTS

Of course, consumer reports have to reach the intended audience, or they have accomplished little. You need to think how to distribute them. Do you ditto them, and pass them around among your associates? Do you write a technical article? (If so, see a succeeding section in this chapter.) Do you write a nontechnical article for a semiprofessional journal? Do you write a ''popular magazine'' piece or a newspaper item? Do you volunteer for a colloquium or seminar? Do you offer your services as an after-dinner speaker?

Report for Other Researchers

Researchers should always share their findings within their fields of study and sometimes in related fields as well. Several modes for doing this are available: (1) a research article, monograph, or book, (2) a report to the "clearinghouse" in your area, e.g. in education the ERIC Clearinghouses accumulate this type of report and publish abstracts and lists to inform readers of what is available, (3) a presentation at a professional meeting, frequently with publication of the paper or at least an abstract in a journal or book of abstracts, e.g. the American Chemical Society publishes all abstracts of papers scheduled for presentation at meetings, (4) an "in house" publication for distribution to a smaller group of selected researchers.

Whatever the mode of presentation, remember that this audience will be most interested in your research design and procedures and in your findings. They probably will care very little to hear about who helped with the work, about budgets, and about your inferences (they are prepared to make their own inferences from your report of what you found). This, then, is a technical report, and the following outline is suggested.

1. Introduction and problem statement. Do not spend a lot of effort to justify the problem, just indicate its origin and context. Perhaps it is part of a larger overall problem that you are studying; perhaps it grew out of a theory you were proposing. Describe the origin briefly, and state the problem very clearly; do not use the terminology, "The purpose of this study was . . . ." State the problem either as a question or as a hypothesis.

2. Backround (literature search). In this section your readers will be interested only in questions such as, "Did the researcher explore the literature completely, with special reference to the latest theories and findings? Was the research based on current, or even forward-looking thought in the field? Were the latest techniques used or, if older techniques were employed, were they justified?" They will not be greatly concerned with reading a detailed explanation of how you narrowed down the problem area or of how you learned a given statistical manipulation (unless it is a unique one that you may have invented). There may be among your audience those who are currently doing research in the same area or in closely related areas; they will be especially concerned whether or not you considered their work, and whether you gave proper credit to them for background utilized in your own study.

The following are recommended for this section: (a) be careful to use the recently published background materials, although you need not describe them in great detail, (b) reference living colleagues who are doing related research, (c) provide evidence, through an extensive bibliography (consider an *annotated* bibliography), that you did a thorough literature search, (d) keep

106

the section short but indicate that a more complete report of the literature search is available elsewhere (in your agency report or in a separate article).

3. Design and procedures. Take special pains to make this section clear and thorough. Think in terms of replication; if a colleague of yours wanted to replicate your study, there should be enough information available in this section of the report to enable him to do so. Include your data analysis methodology also, but avoid too much detail; you can assume that your colleagues will also have the same skills that you have in this area.

This section of your report lays you open to criticism from your colleagues. If you were sloppy in some aspect of the procedures, it will show up; if there were limitations under which you had to work you will not be able to hide them. The best defense being a good offense, then, you need to be careful to describe the limitations and shortcomings of your work in this section. You are not really interested in implying that your research was anything beyond what it really was anyway, so admit problems and tell how you attempted to overcome them.

4. Findings or results. Tell the answer to your original research problem in terms of the data you collected. Indicate the significance and, if necessary, tell how you chose the level of significance. Whether or not you should include actual data is somewhat of a problem. Your readers will be interested in your actual data, but you do not want to take up large amounts of space to present it in this report. If data can be set in tables, this is a good method of presentation. Perhaps you should include partial data to support what you report as findings. You really need to decide how much space you can devote to this effort. In any case, you need to indicate where the original data is stored and to suggest that it will be made available to interested researchers. Tell *how* they may obtain it also.

5. Bibliography. As suggested earlier, this should be extensive. Your colleagues will not only check on your coverage of the field but also, in some cases, they will utilize your bibliography to assist them in their own literature searches.

Article

The primary consideration in preparing an article for possible publication in a research journal should be twofold. (1) the needs of the readers of that journal — this will dictate the content of your article — and (2) the publication guidelines of the journal — this will dictate the format and style. Enough has probably been said already in this chapter about speaking to your audience, so plan your content accordingly. The publication guidelines of the journal may be found in the journal itself or in a separate publication.[2] If you look in the journal, you may find a section, usually on the front or back inside cover, that gives the publication requirements, length of articles, style of manuscript, method of footnoting, number of copies to be supplied, and so forth. Information will commonly be available regarding the obtaining of reprints or extra copies of the journal.

Journals usually select articles for publication through a jury process in which your article may be read by three or four editorial advisors who are specialists in the field of research represented by your article. Their vote will determine whether your article gets published, revised, or rejected. It is probably better to err on the side of including a bit too much detail (so that the editorial board can suggest cutting some of it out) than on the side of being too brief (if they do not understand fully, they may reject instead of asking for more detail).

Generally speaking, you should present your article to only one journal. If it is rejected, then you can revise it and submit it to another potential publisher.

A FEW PERSONAL COMMENTS ON WRITING ARTICLES

From having read many, many research articles, I find that my opinion of the abstracts that usually accompany them is low. I am not sure whether it is the article's author that is to blame in all cases, but often it is the author who is asked to submit an abstract as well as the article manuscript. The abstract is supposed to "whet the interest of readers" so that they will want to read the whole article, but in these times with so much research being available, what most readers want is a very quick survey of the whole project so that they can absorb this information quickly and then move on to other articles for the same purpose. I do not want to have my interest whetted by your abstract, I want to get all of the information I can get from the abstract itself so that, maybe, I can avoid having to read the whole article. I strongly recommend that you write your abstract in the manner that has been suggested in this book.

When I get into reading the article itself, I am turned off by statments of the *purpose*. ("The purpose of this research was to examine the plant succession on abandoned fields in Southern Indiana.") What I want to know is, What was the research *question* that you were trying to answer? Either state this for me in question form or tell me the research hypothesis that you investigated.

I also dislike the inclusion of a kind of literature search in the article; I nearly always skip over these and look for the beginning of your description of what *you* did. The exception is that a research article in my field, in my major professional journal, may *sometimes* contain something in the literature search (often called *background*) section that I want. I suggest that you be very careful in writing this section of your article and consider

[2]Examples of this are the following:

Publication Manual of the American Psychological Association, latest revision, (Washington, D.C., the American Psychological Association).

Style Manual, American Institute of Physics, latest revision, (New York, the American Institue of Physics).

the nature of the journal for which you are writing it. In most cases, I recommend minimizing this section. I also suggest that you make it easy for readers to do what I said I do, to skip over this section and get on with the description of your research. Use subheadings to indicate where your description begins.

Finally, when I read an article, I am most interested in finding out what your answer was to the research question. "What are the facts?" as they used to say in a radio and TV program. I do not care too much what your speculations are, although they are sometimes interesting. They are usually at the end of the article, and I can just stop if I do not want to read them.

A Research Monograph

If you have the opportunity to write a research monograph, you can include all of the things you have been advised to put into any of the preceding publications. Give details, be specific, write in as technical language as you desire, etc. The one thing to be careful of is speculation or drawing inferences. In some monographs this would be strictly forbidden; the purpose would be to present findings in detail and let users make whatever inferences they want to make. In other publications the inclusion of speculation would be a must. The purpose would be to provide a forward move in the field, and the basic way in which this is accomplished is to present the inferences that can be drawn from research so that these inferences can then be "tested" in further research.

A Book

If you have sufficient research information that you want to publish it in book form, it is to be strongly recommended that you *not* prepare the manuscript before having a contract with a specific publisher. In case you are wondering how anyone could obtain enough information from his own research, particularly in a single problem, to merit publishing it in a book, note that this very thing is often the goal of historical research or of anthropological research, and often of others as well. A book mentioned earlier, *The Children of Sanchez* by Oscar Lewis, is a prime example. Do publish the research, or parts of it, in articles first if you can; you will not be losing anything by doing this, since you can then reprint the articles in your book.

The way to begin on a book is to prepare a *prospectus*. Plan your whole book, make an outline in detail, and think of the points to be included in each section of the outline. Then choose a single chapter from somewhere in the outline, choose the one that you will most enjoy writing and on which you think you can do the best job, and write that chapter. Then annotate all of the other chapters, describe their contents in narrative form. Write a preface or introduction to the proposed book in which you explain its purpose, and identify its prospective audience. Update your vita. Finally, write a cover letter to be sent to a publisher, in which you tell what the book is about, to whom it is intended to be addressed, who the prospective buyers might be, and what the competition is, if any.

Put all of this together as follows:

1. A cover giving the title as "Prospectus for . . .," identifying yourself as author and giving the date
2. The cover letter
3. The preface
4. The annotated table of contents
5. The sample chapter
6. Your vita

A variation of this is the following: you may want to take the cover letter out of the prospectus and use it literally as a cover letter addressed individually to the publisher to whom you want to send the materials. As with all of the publications discussed so far, make at least one copy; never send away your only copy of something you have written unless you are willing to have it lost.

Identify potential publishers by looking at numerous books in your field to find out the type of books in which each publisher specializes. Send the prospectus to only one publisher; if it is refused, you can then send it to another.

How do you write a book? This is a question that really cannot be answered here. You must develop your own style. The purpose will dictate much of the manner of presentation. The publisher will have specific requirements. You may work with an editor who will help you to put the ideas into proper form.

A Few Final Details

This chapter closes, now, with the following suggestions or information outlined in several small categories.

COPYRIGHTING

You can copyright your materials simply by stating on the title page the word *copyright* and/or the copyright symbol, a small c with a circle drawn around it, indicating by whom they are copyrighted (yourself, presumably) and giving the date. You can add other statements if you wish, such as, "These materials may not be reproduced in any form except by permission of the author." What is accomplished by indicating that materials are copyrighted is to give notice to users that you are claiming ownership. If you really want to be able to defend your copyright, you must register it with the federal government, the Copyright Office, Library of Congress. You really do not need to do this, however, since the publisher of your article, monograph, or book will do it for you. If your report is shorter than these, your notice as indicated previously will probably be sufficient to keep the materials from being misused.

FOOTNOTING

In a research report there will invariably be a need to give credit to other authors and/or to explain something that the text does not make clear. Footnoting is done in so many ways that this book has avoided specifying any of them as desirable. Perhaps the main rule is to be consistent. Do not mix modes of footnoting in the same paper. A second rule might be not to place in a footnote anything that can legitimately be placed in the text. A third rule might be that explanatory footnotes should be very short.

SPACING

Double-space everything. If in doubt regarding headings, double double-space. It is better to err on the side of too much space than on the side of crowding.

STYLE

Research reports should always be written in impersonal style. Do not say, ''I selected the sample by random techniques.'' Say, ''The sample was selected by random techniques.'' Also, as has been said at least once before, the report is formal. Do not use contractions (such as ''don't''); do not refer to the reader as ''you'' Also, never include levity of any kind.

QUOTING, PARAPHRASING

Ordinarily you should paraphrase the material of others and give credit to the source with some footnoting technique. Sometimes an original statement is so good that you want to use it directly. Quoting is all right in a research report if not carried to an extreme.

Small quotes are simply included within a sentence in the usual fashion, enclosed in quotation marks. See a style manual for introductory phrase suggestions. Long quotations are indented, single-spaced, and are not enclosed in quotation marks. When a quotation is to be used to form a part of one of your own sentences, it is proper to alter a beginning capital or an ending punctuation mark so that it fits properly into your sentence structure. Other than this, a quotation must be presented exactly as it was in the original, including any errors identified if you wish by (sic).

For long quotations you need to obtain permission of the original author or copyright holder.

CORRECTIONS

Theses and dissertations are not supposed to have visible corrections in them. Other manuscripts may be corrected by use of the white xylol solution that is sold under various trade names for ''painting over'' errors. Do not write in corrections, retype the material, except in a manuscript that will be processed through an editor before it goes to the printer for typesetting.

COPIES

Electrostatic copying processes are so inexpensive that they are widely used when small numbers of copies are required. This type of copy is often acceptable even for theses and dissertations (in which case, by the way, you can use correction fluid on the original because the corrections will not show up in the electrostatic copies). For large numbers of copies you need to check with a printer to see if there may be less expensive processes available.

TYPE

Again, these reports are formal. "Formal" type should be used. It is a little hard to tell what this means, except that you should not use script type, for example, or any of the fancy or large-or small-size types that are now available. Plain, blocky type with pica or elite spacing should be used for safety (so your paper does not get rejected on this account).

DIAGRAMS, PHOTOGRAPHS, AND OTHER ILLUSTRATIONS

Diagrams and anything else not produced with the typewriter need to be drawn with India ink. It is possible, however, to include photographs and drawings copied electrostatically. You really need the help of a printer for this, so if you are planning to go beyond drawing your own diagrams with India ink, check with an expert. You had better also check with whoever has to approve your paper to make sure that such pictures will be acceptable.

OUTSIZE INSERTS

Occasionally you might need a large map or blueprint or something else that will not fit into the regular size of your report and that will not be acceptable if photographically reduced. The usual rule is that either it has to be folded to fit within the bounds of the rest of the paper for edge binding or it has to be folded and placed in a pocket in an appendix.

BINDING

Do not use paper clips; bind your papers in some way. Staple thin papers at the upper left corner. Even better would be to place a cover on them and staple them along the left margin. Do not use the plastic covers with slip-on backs; the papers come apart too easily. For thick papers, use a professional binding, not a loose-leaf or spring-back folder. The general idea is to make the paper sturdy and permanent so that pages will not get lost. You also want it to be easily handled by the reader and easily stored in a file or bookcase.

So, there you have it. You have carried out a piece of research all the way from the initial thinking stage, through a proposal, through setting up the apparatus and collecting information through data analysis, to a report (or reports). No doubt you are tired of the topic of this first research, but that will not last. The thrill of seeing others use your findings will be so great that you will be at it again in no time. Research breeds more research. Good luck!

By the way, remember all the talk about serendipity in research? Also, remember the opening story about the scientist who discovered how robins find earthworms? Suppose he had seen an earthworm like the one in the final cartoon in this book!

INDEX